FIONA CULLEN

The Smugglers' Caves

CORNELSEN **ENGLISH** LIBRARY

Cornelsen

Cornelsen English Library
Fiona Cullen · The Smugglers' Caves

Verlagsredaktion
Michael Dunkel

Umschlaggestaltung
hawemannundmosch, Konzeption und Gestaltung, Berlin

Titelbild
David Hudson / fotoLibra, Harlech

Illustration
Jan Stoewe, München

Layout
Buchgestaltung+, Berlin

Technische Umsetzung
Buch und Gestaltung – Britta Dieterle, Berlin

Passende Arbeitsblätter und weitere Hilfen zu diesem Titel gibt es unter:
www.cornelsen.de/cel

www.cornelsen.de

1. Auflage, 6. Druck 2022

Alle Drucke dieser Auflage sind inhaltlich unverändert und können im Unterricht nebeneinander verwendet werden.

Druck: AZ Druck und Datentechnik GmbH, Kempten

ISBN 978-3-06-032951-9

PEFC/04-31-2260

PEFC zertifiziert
Dieses Produkt stammt aus nachhaltig bewirtschafteten Wäldern und kontrollierten Quellen.

www.pefc.de

Contents

Chapter 1 Beth moves in

When Jack got home from school on the last day of the summer term, Beth was there. She was mopping the kitchen floor. It was just a few weeks after Jack's mum's funeral.

Beth was wearing a slinky, low-cut dress and high-heeled silver sandals. The smell of her perfume was sweet and heavy.

Jack ran into the kitchen to get a cold drink from the fridge. He slipped on the wet floor and fell.

"What do you want, Jack?" Beth asked.

Jack ignored her question. "Why are you here?" he asked.

"Well, I was your mum's best friend. I'm going to look after you and your dad."

"You weren't my mum's best friend," said Jack.

He took a roll of bin bags out of a drawer. He tore a bin bag off the roll. Then he went up to his mum and dad's bedroom. The door was shut. It had never been shut before. Jack opened it and went in. He knelt down in front of his mum's bedside cabinet and opened it. He was going to put his mum's medicine in the bin bag. Then he was going to take the medicine to a chemist's to get rid of it. He wanted to remember his mum, not his mum's cancer.

But the medicine had gone. There were lipsticks, eye shadows and bottles of perfume in the bedside cabinet now. Jack's mum had never used make-up or perfume.

He went down to the living room to see what was on TV. He opened the living room door – another door that had never been shut before. The photos on the mantelpiece had gone. His mum and dad's photo had gone. The photo of his mum and him when he was a baby had gone, too.

Jack was staring at the empty mantelpiece when he suddenly smelt Beth's perfume. He heard her voice behind him.

"Oh, Jack, look at the mud on the carpet. This room is too nice for kids. It should be a grown-ups' room."

Jack didn't turn around. He waited until Beth had left the room. Then he went through the hall to the front door and left the house.

Joy, who lived next door, came out of her house and saw him. She put some empty cardboard packets in her green wheelie bin.

"Come and have something to eat with us, Jack," Joy said as she shut the bin. "We're having garlic bread with prawns and tomatoes. I bought lots of prawns today."

Jack followed her into her house, number 27 Collier Road.

They went into the kitchen. Jack sat down at the table next to Joy's foster daughter, Madeleine. Madeleine hugged him. Her new hair extensions brushed his face.

"Hi," she said.

"Hi," said Jack into her hair extensions.

"Steve, you haven't said hi to Jack," said Madeleine to a thin boy with spiked-up hair.

"Hi," said Steve between mouthfuls of garlic bread.

"Hi, Steve," said Jack.

"Are you going to gel your hair like Steve's?" asked Madeleine. "It's the holidays, so we can have any hairstyle we like for the next six weeks."

"No, I don't think so," said Jack.

Steve was putting prawns into his mouth as fast as he could. Madeleine was eating more slowly.

"Do you have prawns in Zimbabwe, Madeleine?" Jack asked.

"No, Zimbabwe's a long way from the sea," she answered.

Steve put a last prawn into his mouth and stood up. He started walking towards the kitchen door.

"Don't you have river prawns?" Jack asked Madeleine.

"Well, we do, but our government killed a lot of people. Their bodies were thrown into the rivers. So people stopped eating fish and prawns from the rivers. I don't know if they do now ... Hey, Steve, don't go. You and I are washing up today."

Joy said, "Shall we go up on the balcony, Jack?"

Jack followed Joy into the hall. Steve watched them. He looked sad.

Joy and Jack went upstairs to a bedroom at the back of the house. Like Jack's own bedroom, this room had a small balcony.

Jack and Joy stood on the balcony together.

"Mum used to come up and stand on my balcony every night when it got dark," said Jack. "She liked looking down at the lights of the fishing boats. And she liked looking over at the West Hill and down at the Old Town."

"Yes, she loved this view," said Joy. "Jack ... Beth has been at your place all day today, hasn't she?"

"Yes. I hate her. She hates me, too. I didn't mind so much about the nights. She started coming to stay the night when Mum was in the hospice. She came to the house late at night when she thought I was asleep. But now she's there in the daytime as well."

"Have you told your dad how you feel?"

"I haven't had a chance. He's been working a lot."

"Well, don't let her take over. Invite your friends to your house like you did when your mum was alive."

The cordless phone on the bedroom mantelpiece started ringing.

"Wait there a moment, Jack," said Joy. She left the balcony and went to answer the phone.

"Hi," Jack heard her say. "You don't usually phone me in the evening, Chris ... Oh, I see. How old is he? ... Yes, thirteen is fine, but I'll only take refugee or asylum seeker kids from now on. The English kids are too traumatized ... Yes, I know Madeleine lost everything, but her parents were killed. They didn't abandon her ... No, Chris, I really can't take another rejected kid at the moment. Steve is still frightened ... When Madeleine came to me, Steve was jealous and scared ... No, I mean it. I can't, Chris ... Well, phone me again if you can't place him one-to-one. Or e-mail me ... Yes ... OK, yes, I could come and talk to him ... Yes, let me know ... Bye, Chris."

As she put the phone down, Jack came in from the balcony. He said he was going home.

They went downstairs. Joy opened the front door and said, "Remember, Jack – invite your friends to your house. Starting from tomorrow."

Chapter 2 The hidden passageway

The next morning at breakfast, Jack said to his dad, "Is it all right if I have a few people round this morning?"

"Of course it is. Enjoy your morning," said his dad.

"I'll make some more toast," said Beth. She stood up and went to put some bread in the toaster. She stroked Jack's dad's hair as she passed his chair.

Jack's dad nudged him and passed him a £20 note under the table. Jack took the money and smiled his thanks, but he was worried. Why did his dad feel that he had to give him money behind Beth's back?

Just after Jack's dad had driven off, the doorbell rang. Beth answered it. It was the meter reader.

"Jack!" Beth shouted. "Where's the electricity meter?"

Jack came into the hall and said it was in the cellar. Beth took the cellar key off a hook on the hall wall and handed it to him. Jack was surprised that she knew it was the cellar key.

"Right, Jack will take you down and show you the meter, won't you, Jack?" said Beth.

"Yes, it's this way," Jack said to the man. He led him out into the back garden and over the patio to the cellar door.

Jack unlocked the door and left the key in it.

The man bent his head under the door frame and followed Jack in.

The man got out a torch and switched it on. The light from the torch was powerful.

Jack led the man to an alcove in the side wall near the back of the cellar. The meter was in the alcove. The man squeezed between the side wall and an old wardrobe. The wardrobe was standing against the back wall of the cellar. There were spiders' webs hanging between the wardrobe and the walls.

The man ducked down and went into the alcove. When he had read the meter, he came out again. He shone his torch on the wardrobe.

"If we move this wardrobe, it'll be easier for me to get in next time," he said. "Old George is thinner than me."

"Who's Old George?"

"He's the man who used to read the meters in this road. He retired last month. He could get into any small space."

They pushed the wardrobe. It fell sideways onto the ground.

"What's behind that hole?" the man asked. He was shining his torch on a large, roundish hole in the back wall. The hole had been hidden by the wardrobe.

"I don't know," said Jack.

"So you didn't even know there was a hole there," said the man. He took a little torch out of a pocket in his uniform jacket. "Well, I must go. Here, you have my pocket torch. You can keep it. I don't need it. It's just a spare. Use it to check out the hole."

Jack took the small torch from the meter man. He switched it on. The light from it was surprisingly powerful.

"The lady up in the house isn't your mum, is she?" the man said as they made their way to the cellar door.

"No."

"Is this her broomstick?" The man pointed at an old-fashioned broom near the door. "I bet you wish she would fly away on it."

"Yes, I do ... Thanks for the torch," said Jack as the man left the cellar.

The man waved and walked round the side of the house.

Jack returned to the back wall. He shone the torch on it and ran his hands over its surface. It wasn't made of brick like the other walls in the cellar. It was a sandstone wall. Jack could feel the grains of sand under his fingers.

The hole was quite high up, so he looked around for something to stand on. Then he remembered that there was a wooden box next to the broom. He went back to the cellar entrance to get it.

When he got there, the cellar door was shut. Jack pushed it, but it wouldn't open.

"Let me out!" he shouted through the door. "Hey, I'm in here."

He heard footsteps above him on the floorboards of the ground floor of the house. He shouted upwards. But nobody came.

Beth must have locked him in.

He took out his mobile to phone his dad. Then he remembered that he hadn't topped it up.

He lifted up the wooden box. It was quite heavy, so he put it down again. He opened it, thinking he could take something out to make it lighter.

He shone the torch inside. There was a photo of his mum and dad on their wedding day in the box. And there was a photo of his mum and him when he was a baby. They were the photos that had disappeared from the mantelpiece. His mum's jewellery box with her wedding ring and her earrings and bracelets in it was under the photos.

Beth must have brought his mum's things down to the cellar and put them in the wooden box near the entrance door.

Jack felt really angry with Beth. But he was glad he had found his mum's things. He closed the box, dragged it to the back wall and stood on it. Then he shone the torch through the hole. He saw a sandstone passageway on the other side.

He knew he could turn around and squeeze backwards through the hole. Then he could drop to the ground on the other side. But he wanted the wooden box with him in the passageway.

He went to a part of the cellar where his dad kept boxes of firewood and dragged one of the boxes to the back wall. It was only a cardboard box, but it was filled with logs. He stood on the logs. Then he lifted the wooden box to the hole and pushed it through. The things inside it jangled as it fell to the floor of the passageway.

Jack squeezed backwards through the hole. He was still holding the little torch as he dropped to the ground on the other side.

He left the wooden box on the ground by the wall and started to walk along the passageway. It was quite narrow, but he didn't have to bend like he did in the cellar.

The passageway went on for ages. Then it started to widen out until he was in a small cavern. At first, Jack thought the cavern had probably been formed naturally by the sea. But then he saw a narrow flight of steps carved into the sandstone over on his left.

He went over to the steps. As he started going down them, he could hear voices. They were coming from below, from beyond the bottom of the steps. They were young voices, laughing, talking and shouting.

At the bottom, there was a very narrow opening in the rock. Jack saw a small briefcase on the ground. He thought it was a strange place to put a briefcase. There was a chain

tied to its handle and a blue sticker in the shape of a cat on the side. The cat was stretching. It had sharp front claws. Jack decided he could look at the briefcase later. He squeezed through the opening.

Jack looked up and saw two waxwork smugglers and a boat. He moved forwards out of the shadows.

"Come out of there!" a woman shouted.

Jack switched off his torch. He edged his way round the boat to where the woman was standing. There was a wooden sign in front of the boat. It said Midnight Landing.

The woman was wearing a sweatshirt with the Hastings Attractions Smugglers Adventure logo on it.

"Are you all right?" she asked.

"I'm fine," said Jack. "Sorry ..."

"Oh, that's OK. Off you go. Follow the arrows."

Jack followed the arrows on the walls. He passed a group of Italian teenagers. They were shooting at wooden smugglers from a rifle range.

He reached the souvenir shop near the exit. His friend Dave was sitting near the cash desk. Dave lived in Collier Road, too. He was at the same school as Jack, Madeleine and Steve. Dave's dad worked at the Smugglers Adventure tourist attraction in the caves. Dave often went there to work with him in the holidays.

Dave's dad was taking money from the souvenir buyers. Dave was sticking prices onto rolled-up maps of the caves. Dave was blind. But he was having no problem sticking the prices on the maps.

Jack went over to Dave.

"Hi, Dave. It's me, Jack," said Jack.

"Oh, hi," said Dave. "Who's with you?"

"Nobody," said Jack.

"If I had known you were here, I would have gone around the caves with you," said Dave.

"I'll come again," said Jack. "I went around really quickly today. I'll come back tomorrow. I'll see if Madeleine and Steve from next door want to come."

"Come to the shop tomorrow and I'll go around with you."

"OK, see you then," said Jack.

Jack left the souvenir shop and went out through the exit gate. He walked along the path and up the steps to the grass on the West Hill.

He walked over the grass to Collier Road and then ran to Joy's house. He wanted to tell Madeleine and Steve about the passageway. He rang the bell. Nobody came to the door. So he went to his own front door and unlocked it. As he walked into the hall, Beth came out of the living room.

"Jack," she said, staring at him.

He walked past her into the kitchen. He made himself a cheese sandwich and a cup of tea and took them upstairs to his room. Beth had gone back into the living room and shut the door.

Jack sat at his desk to eat his sandwich. When he had finished it, he took his cup of tea onto his balcony. He looked down at the fishing beach as he sipped his tea. Then he looked down at the garden. Some sparrows were eating ants from the sandy cracks in the patio.

Suddenly, the sparrows flew up from the patio and over into the hedge. Beth appeared in the garden. She walked over the patio to the cellar door. She stared at the door. She pulled it, but it didn't open. Then she turned to walk back to the side of the house.

Jack picked up the phone on his desk and phoned Steve's mobile.

"Steve, it's me," he said. "Can you and Madeleine come to my house tomorrow? ... Yes? ... Yes, after breakfast. I've got something to show you ... Yes. Right, see you then."

Chapter 3 The smugglers' caves

Steve and Madeleine went to Jack's house after breakfast the next morning.

Jack let them in. He took the cellar key from its hook and led them into the back garden. He unlocked the cellar door and switched his torch on. Steve and Madeleine followed him to the back of the cellar.

"Look at that," Jack said. He shone his torch at the hole in the sandstone wall.

"I'll show you where I was yesterday," he said. He climbed on the box of firewood.

One by one, they followed. They squeezed backwards through the hole. Then they dropped onto the sandstone floor of the passageway on the other side.

"Does this passageway lead anywhere?" asked Steve.

"It goes to the Smugglers Adventure," said Jack.

"I've heard of the Smugglers Adventure, but I've never been in," said Madeleine as she followed Jack down the passageway. "Hey, Steve, aren't you coming with us?"

Steve was standing still by the hole in the wall. He took a deep breath and started following them.

"Are you OK, Steve?" asked Madeleine.

"Yes, I'm OK," he said.

When they reached the narrow opening, Jack stopped and said, "There was a briefcase here yesterday. But it's gone. It was on a chain. Someone must have pulled it through. Oh, well, let's go and find Dave."

"Does he know about the passageway?" asked Steve.

"Not yet. We'll tell him. But we won't tell anyone else, OK?"

"Not even Joy?" asked Madeleine.

"Well, maybe Joy. But nobody else. Come on. We'll get Dave and then we'll go around the caves. We'll be like all the foreign students and tourists."

They squeezed through the opening. Jack switched off his torch. There was a group of French students near the smugglers' boat. Jack, Madeleine and Steve crouched in the shadows. When the French students had gone, Madeleine and Steve followed Jack through the caves to the souvenir shop.

When they got there, Dave was rolling up a poster for a French student. Dave's dad was hanging plastic skeletons on a display stand.

Madeleine waited until the student had taken the poster. Then she leaned over the counter and kissed Dave on the cheek.

"Hi, Madeleine," said Dave.

"How did you know it was me?"

"The beads on your hair extensions hit my face."

"We're not busy at the moment," said Dave's dad. "So you can go around the caves with your friends if you want, Dave."

Dave came around to them from behind the counter.

"Guide me over to the cave wall and I'll feel my way around with you. Put my left hand on the wall," he said.

Madeleine guided him to the cave wall. She put his hand on the sandstone. As they walked, Jack told Dave about the passageway from his cellar to the caves.

"That's cool," said Dave. "I knew there were lots of passageways. But I thought the town council had blocked them all up."

"So did I," said Steve. "Dave ..."

"Yes?"

"It's very dark in here."

"We sell torches at the entrance," said Dave. "But we don't have too much lighting. It should be spooky."

"Oh, right," said Steve.

"We're passing the interactive zone, Dave," said Madeleine. "Some children are pressing buttons to find out what the smugglers used to smuggle."

"Tea, sugar, spices, paper, silk, leather, jewellery, alcohol and tobacco. I know the list by heart," said Dave.

"We're looking at some waxworks of drunken smugglers now," said Madeleine.

"Are they moving?" asked Dave.

"Yes, one is raising his drink and lowering it," said Jack.

"Ah, right ... It's good to get a picture of everything. Dad tries to make time to describe the things he can see. But he's often too busy. This morning, I heard a dog whining. I was near the bottom of the entrance tunnel, the passage they call the Monks' Walk. I asked Dad if there was a whining dog waxwork there. He said there wasn't."

"Maybe someone brought a dog in."

"No, dogs aren't allowed in here – apart from guide dogs," said Dave. "What can you see now?"

"A dead smuggler hanging from a gibbet."

"Oh, yes. They started hanging smugglers in the mid-1700s," said Dave. "Ah, we're in the chapel now."

"The chapel? How do you know?"

"Because it's always so cold in the chapel. I suppose it's cold because it's so deep down. But they say it's haunted. Nobody knows why it's called the chapel."

He felt his way round the walls of the chapel until he came to a huge shape carved in the sandstone.

"That's a spooky-looking carving," said Jack. "It's a person with horns, Dave."

"I think it's a very old carving of a pagan god," said Dave's dad, who had just come into the chapel.

"Do you need me in the shop, Dad?" Dave asked.

"Not yet. No, I just wanted to ask you something: did Mum bring my Shakespeare costume?"

"Yes, she put it under the counter in the shop."

"Great. Thanks."

Dave's dad turned and made his way back to the souvenir shop.

Dave led Madeleine, Jack and Steve out of the chapel.

"Oh, that's a bit warmer," said Madeleine. "You were in a hurry to get out of there, Steve."

"It was too cold and dark," said Steve.

"What was your dad talking about, Dave?" asked Madeleine. "What Shakespeare costume?"

"Oh, my mum and dad give talks to foreign students and tourists. The talks are about famous people. Mum and Dad dress up as the famous people when they give the talks. They're giving a talk on Shakespeare this evening."

"Shall we go out on the hill now?" interrupted Steve.

"Steve, you're shivering," said Madeleine. "Yes, let's go out on the hill."

As they went through the tunnels and caverns to the exit, Jack continued to tell Dave what he could see.

"Now we're looking at a skeleton. There are rags hanging off it. There's a dagger in its ribs."

"Oh, that's the traitor," said Dave. "That's cool."

"Let's *go*," pleaded Steve.

Chapter 4 Memories of the dark

Jack, Madeleine and Steve squinted as they went out into the sunlight. Dave's mum was sitting at the ticket office near the entrance. As they left through the exit, she said hello.

"You don't need me, do you, Mum?" said Dave.

"Not at the moment. I can watch the shop and the exit from here. It's great that the entrance and exit gates are beside each other. I can see everyone going in and out."

Madeleine took Steve's arm as they went up the steps to the grass.

"Are you OK now?" she asked.

"I don't feel great," Steve said. "I think I'll go home."

"I'll go with you," said Madeleine.

"No, you stay," said Steve. "I'll see you later." He left. The others sat down on the grass.

"I think Steve wants to be on his own with Joy for a while," said Madeleine.

"He got scared in the caves," said Dave. "Is the dark really so scary for sighted people?"

"It depends on your memories of the dark," said Madeleine. "I liked the dark of the Chinhoyi Caves in Zimbabwe. I hid there. Some of our caves have holes in the roof. The sun shines through the holes. And one cave has electric lights for tourists. But I hid in the caves that didn't have any light. I felt safer in the dark. I didn't want anyone to find me."

"Has Steve got bad memories of the dark?" asked Dave.

"Yes, he has," said Jack. "Probably he'll tell you about it sometime ..."

"Jack," interrupted Madeleine. "Tell Dave about the briefcase."

"Oh, right … I found a briefcase yesterday. It was by the opening leading from my passageway into the Smugglers Adventure. It had a blue cat sticker on the side."

"So someone else knows about your passageway," said Dave.

"No, I don't think so," said Jack. "I think someone pushed it through from the Smugglers Adventure side. And someone pulled it back later. There was a chain attached to it to pull it through with. Probably they think it's just a hole in the cave wall where they can hide their briefcase. I don't think they know there's a passageway … Dave, your dad's coming up the steps."

"It's probably time to get back to work," said Dave. "Hi, Dad."

"Hi. Can you help in the shop now?"

"Yes, sure. Has the group of Italians arrived?"

"Yes, they've just gone in."

"Right, I'm coming. See you, Madeleine. See you, Jack."

"See you, Dave."

"Can I come back to your house for a while, Jack?" asked Madeleine. "I want to give Steve a bit of time alone with Joy."

"Sure," said Jack.

Chapter 5 House rules

Jack turned his front door key in the lock. He pushed the door, but it wouldn't open. It was bolted from the inside.

He rang the bell.

"Sorry, Madeleine," he said. "It's bolted."

"Does your dad normally bolt the door?"

"No."

He rang the bell again.

They heard the bolt being drawn back.

Beth stood with the door slightly open.

"Hello, Jack," she said.

"Hi."

"You've got a friend with you."

"Yes."

"I didn't know you were planning to have a friend around today."

"Beth, we can't get in with you holding the door like that," said Jack.

Beth let go of the door and went upstairs.

Jack and Madeleine went in.

"Do you want a sandwich?" Jack asked.

"Yes, that would be great," Madeleine said. "I'm hungry."

She followed him into the kitchen. Jack made two cheese sandwiches. He put them on two plates on a tray.

"Let's see what's on TV," he said.

Madeleine followed him to the living room. Jack handed her the tray so that he could open the living room door.

Then he saw that there was a padlock on the door.

The bottom stair creaked. Jack turned around. Beth was standing at the bottom of the stairs. Her arms were folded.

She was wearing a short black dress with a red belt. Her fingernails and toenails were painted red. They matched her belt and her shiny red high-heeled sandals.

"Well, you have to have house rules," she said. "The living room is too nice for kids."

Jack sat down on the hall floor.

"We'll have our sandwiches here, then," he said.

Madeleine sat down beside him.

"You can sit at the kitchen table," said Beth. "You'll get crumbs on the hall carpet if you sit here."

"Mmm, these sandwiches are yummy. What did you put in them, Jack?" asked Madeleine.

"Cheese and pickle," said Jack.

"Ah, pickle. I'd heard of it, but I've never had it before," said Madeleine.

Beth turned away and went upstairs. As she turned, a folded sheet of paper fell out of a little side pocket in her dress. Jack picked it up. He pushed it into his jeans pocket.

"The caves brought back bad memories for Steve, didn't they?" said Madeleine. "Did he tell you ...?"

"Yes, he told me after my mum died. He said that his mum and dad were drug addicts. They went out one evening, took a lot of drugs and ended up staying out for three days. They lost track of time. Steve said the nights were really frightening. He was only four years old. And he couldn't turn the light on because the electricity had been cut off in the flat. I don't know why his mum and dad locked him in."

"They probably thought he would be safer if he were locked in."

"It's strange that the neighbours didn't do anything."

"Well, you hear children shouting and crying sometimes. I don't think the neighbours realized Steve was on his own. They phoned the police on the third night."

"Yes, Steve told me that. There were a lot of drugs raids in the town after that. Joy told me. She said the police arrested quite a lot of people."

"Steve was rescued ten years ago. But he was really scared in the caves today. Do you think people ever get over stuff like that?" asked Jack.

"I think we put on a brave face most of the time. Sometimes when Joy hugs me when there's nobody else around, I feel reassured. I feel as if I'll stop being frightened one day. But then Steve comes in, and I stop hugging Joy. Steve gets jealous."

"You don't look frightened."

"You have to keep going, don't you? If I do really well, maybe they'll let me stay here. Do you know how I came to England? A woman found me in the Chinhoyi Caves. She took me to her house for a few days. She told me she would take me to a good boarding school in England. She said that Mugabe's soldiers wouldn't find me there. Well, I went with her – I didn't know what else to do. Anyway, we flew to England and landed at Heathrow. And the airport officials recognized her. She had brought several girls in before. The officials stopped us before we went through customs. They took me into an office to interview me. After a long interview, I was taken to Joy's house. I had more interviews and they said I can stay here till I'm eighteen. After my eighteenth birthday, they could deport me. But if I do really well at school, maybe they'll let me stay. I don't know what happened to the woman who brought me to England."

"Hang on, Madeleine. I'm a bit lost. What did you mean when you said the woman had brought in several girls before? And why were you hiding in the caves?"

But Madeleine didn't get a chance to tell him more because Jack's dad came in.

"Hi, Dad!" Jack said. "I was trying to phone you."

As Madeleine and Jack stood up, Beth came into the hall and kissed Jack's dad.

Jack's dad put his bag down.

"Is the hot water on?" he asked. "I need a shower."

"I'll go and run you a nice hot bath," said Beth, touching his cheek.

"Thanks," he said as she went upstairs. He took his mobile phone out of his bag. He attached it to a charger that was plugged into a socket in the hall.

"Why aren't you two in the living room?" asked Jack's dad. He went to the living room door and turned the handle. Then he saw the padlock.

"Beth says it's a grown-ups' room. It's too nice for kids," said Jack.

"I'd better go now," said Madeleine.

"OK," said Jack.

He followed Madeleine out of the house.

"See you later, Dad," he shouted.

"Are you going to Madeleine's house?" his dad shouted from the hall.

"No, I'm going to top up my mobile at the shop round the corner. I'll be back soon," said Jack.

Chapter 6 The disappearing briefcase

"I've put your receipt in the bag," Dave said to the last Italian student in the souvenir shop.

"A receipt for an English plate?" asked the Italian girl. She sneezed and blew her nose.

"No, for the bracelet you just bought."

The Italian girl sneezed again.

"My friend means is the receipt for how to cook an English dish?" said an Italian boy.

"Oh, I see. No, not a recipe. A receipt."

"Ah, yes. A receipt. But I only have a cold," said the girl. "And you are not a doctor."

"No, not a prescription. A receipt. For your money."

"Ah, OK, thank you." The girl sneezed again. She and her friend went to the exit gate.

Dave's dad came up to the counter.

"Dave, it's me," he said. "I'll just get my costume. It's under the counter."

"Here you are," said Dave. He reached down and pulled out a large plastic bag of clothes.

"Thanks," said his dad. "I'll go and put it on. Oh, hang on. You've got a couple of customers. Hello, boys."

"Hello," said a German boy. "When do I become the frog?"

"When a wicked witch casts a spell on you," said Dave's dad.

The boy looked confused.

"I ordered a frog the day before yesterday," he said. "I paid for it. When do I become it?"

"You mean, 'When do I get it?'" said Dave.

"Ah, OK." The boy smiled. "I understand now. The prince became a frog when a witch cast a spell on him."

"Here's your frog," said Dave.

He reached under the counter. He took out a large painted wooden frog. It had the Smugglers Adventure logo on its chest.

"I just need your receipt."

"Receipt?"

"The piece of paper we gave you when you paid."

"Ah, OK." The boy put a receipt in Dave's hand.

When they had gone, Dave's dad said, "Let's go out in the fresh air for a few minutes."

They left the caves and went outside onto the path.

"You're looking forward to being Shakespeare tonight, aren't you, Dad?" said Dave. "Are you going to sit in the Shakespeare Tree?"

"Yes. And Mum's going to join me there. She's going to dress up as Lady Macbeth."

"Did Shakespeare ever come to Hastings?"

"I don't think so. But there is a connection. The Shakespeare Tree was grown from a cutting from a mulberry tree. And the mulberry tree was growing in Stratford-upon-Avon in Shakespeare's time ... Oh, your mobile."

Dave answered his vibrating mobile.

"Oh, hi, Jack ... What? ... Yeah, we're still open ... OK, right, I'm on my way. See you soon, Jack."

Dave turned to his dad and said, "Dad, is it OK if I go and meet Jack? He's going to come to the smugglers' boat. You know, the Midnight Landing boat."

"You could meet him at the entrance instead."

"Er ... no, we agreed to meet at the boat."

"OK, that's fine. There are no more big groups booked. And Mum is in the caves somewhere – she can look after the shop. Come down to the Shakespeare Tree with Jack this evening if you want. Here, get yourselves some fish and chips on the way." Dave's dad handed him some money.

"Thanks," said Dave.

They went back into the Smugglers Adventure and climbed over the exit gate. Dave's dad guided Dave through the souvenir shop into the caves. He left him in the tunnel that led from the shop. Dave felt his way through the passageways and caverns that he knew so well. He soon came to the Midnight Landing alcove where the waxwork smugglers stood with their boat.

"Dave, I'm here," Jack whispered.

Jack took Dave's arm and guided him behind the boat to the opening in the cave wall.

Dave squeezed through the opening after Jack.

"If you turn around, you can sit on the steps," said Jack. "I'll sit on the floor."

"The briefcase is here, isn't it?" said Dave. "I felt it just now with my foot."

"Yes."

"You don't sound very interested in it."

"No."

"But you seem to like it here. You've come back again so soon," said Dave as he sat down.

"Well, I can't sit in our living room any more. Beth has padlocked it. So when Madeleine left my house, I decided to go down to the passageway. I keep my mum's photos there. I wanted to look at them. I went to the shop and topped up my mobile first. Then I went home and got the cellar key. I went through the cellar to the hole at the back.

But then I heard Dad shouting my name. I shouted back. But he didn't hear me. I think he was out on the street. I went to the cellar door. But it was locked again. I shouted, but I couldn't hear anyone up in the house. I phoned Dad, but there was no answer. He probably left his mobile in the house. I realized that the only way to get out of the cellar was through the caves. So I phoned you to check they were still open."

Dave suddenly grabbed Jack's arm. "What's that?" he whispered.

"What?"

"Sssh."

Jack listened and heard a jangling sound. He shone his torch down to where the sound was coming from. The briefcase was moving upwards. Someone was pulling the chain from the other side.

Jack switched off his torch. The briefcase disappeared through the opening. Jack put his finger on Dave's lips for a moment. Dave nodded.

After a while, Dave said, "I think they've gone."

Jack switched on his torch and moved over to the opening. He looked through.

He could only see the shadows of the boat and the waxworks.

"Yes, they've gone," he said.

"OK, let's go," said Dave.

Jack put Dave's hand on the opening.

"You go first. I'll follow you," said Dave.

Jack switched his torch off. He squeezed through the opening. Dave followed him. There was no sign of the person who had pulled the briefcase through the opening.

They made their way to the souvenir shop.

"Just in time, you two," said Dave's mum. She came out from behind the till. "We're closing. Trevor wanted to go and look for you. But he had to get ready for the Shakespeare thing."

"Trevor?" said Jack.

"Trevor is my dad's name," said Dave. "Do you want to come and hear Dad being Shakespeare?"

"OK," said Jack. "I can't go anywhere else. I can't even watch TV at home now."

"Dad has given me money for fish and chips," said Dave. "See you, Mum."

"OK. I'll be down later," said Dave's mum.

As they came out of the caves and onto the path, Jack's mobile vibrated.

"Are you OK?" It was a text from his dad.

"Am OK. Going for fish'n'chips with Dave," Jack texted back.

They went down one of the pathways to the Old Town.

"Where shall we get the fish and chips?" asked Dave.

"Webbe's Restaurant, maybe. It's not too far from the Shakespeare Tree."

"OK."

As they went into the restaurant and joined the queue, Dave's dad was coming out with a bag of fish and chips. He was wearing short green trousers, green tights, shoes with buckles, a green jacket, a false beard and a beret with a huge feather in it.

"Hi!" he said. "I'll see you two at the Shakespeare Tree."

Chapter 7 Lady Macbeth's hands

Jack and Dave came out of Webbe's with their fish and chips half an hour later. Madeleine and Steve were waiting outside.

"I didn't expect to see you here. Have a chip," Jack said to them. "Madeleine and Steve are here, Dave."

"Your dad came to our house, Jack," said Steve. "He was looking for you. And then you texted him. He read the text to us. So we came to find you."

"Right, let's go to the Shakespeare Tree," said Jack. "I hope we haven't missed your dad's talk, Dave."

They went up an old street called Courthouse Street. They stopped in a courtyard between two blocks of modern flats. There was a low wall between the two blocks of flats and an enormous mulberry tree on the other side of the wall. The bottom of the tree was in another courtyard two or three metres below. Madeleine took Dave's hand. She guided him past some Japanese students to the wall.

"You are looking at the remains of the thirteenth-century town wall," a voice was saying. The voice belonged to Dave's dad. He was sitting on a branch among the shiny dark green leaves of the mulberry tree. There was half a chip in his false beard.

Two American tourists came and stood near the wall. They asked a Japanese student to take a photo of them. They wanted a photo with Dave's dad in the Shakespeare tree in the background.

Dave's dad stopped talking. He smiled for the camera.

Then he said, "Where was I? I told you about the wall, didn't I? Yes … Now, if you look behind you, my friends, you will see a character from one of Shakespeare's famous tragedies ..."

The tourists and students turned round. They saw Dave's mum. She was wearing a long dark grey dress and a thin black scarf.

"This is Lady Macbeth," said Dave's dad. He bent forwards over a branch that reached as far as the old wall. He clambered over the wall and stood up.

Dave's mum walked over to the wall. She was staring down at her hands in horror. She turned and stood with her back to the wall. Then she held up the palms of her hands. They were dripping with bright red fake blood. The group stared at them.

"I will never get this blood off my hands!" shouted Dave's mum.

"What did your dad call her?" Jack asked Dave.

"Lady Macbeth. The play is called Macbeth."

"Oh, right. All I heard was the Beth bit. OK, so Lady Macbeth has got blood on her hands and she can't wash it off ... a bit like Beth in our house. She's always cleaning. And she's always moaning about mess."

"I can't wash the blood off my hands!" shouted Dave's mum. "The king had so much blood!"

"What's your mum talking about, Dave?" Steve asked.

"Well, Macbeth and his wife, Lady Macbeth, wanted to be king and queen. Macbeth was next in line to the throne. So Lady Macbeth encouraged her husband to murder the king."

"And did he? Did Macbeth kill the king?"

"Yes. Macbeth and his wife invited the king to stay the night with them after a banquet. And when everyone was asleep, Macbeth went into the king's bedroom and stabbed the king."

"Will these hands never be clean?" shouted Dave's mum. She lifted her palms again. She sniffed her right palm.

"My hand smells of blood," she moaned. "No perfume can take the smell away."

"If her husband killed the king, why has Lady Macbeth got blood on her hands?" asked Steve.

"Because she put some of the dead king's blood on the guards' swords. She wanted everyone to think the guards murdered the king."

"But why didn't the guards stop Macbeth from killing the king?"

"Because Lady Macbeth had got them drunk. So they were fast asleep. And Macbeth killed them before they could tell anyone they didn't do it. He said he killed them out of love for the king."

"That's a cool story," said Steve.

Chapter 8 The flashing light

Jack unlocked his front door and pushed it open.

Dave, Madeleine and Steve followed Jack into the hall. They all went upstairs to his bedroom.

Beth came out of the living room and shouted up the stairs, "What's going on, Jack?"

"I've brought some friends home. Where's Dad?"

Jack's dad came out of the living room.

"Hi, Jack,"' he shouted up the stairs.

"Hi, Dad. Come up to my room."

"Maybe later, OK?"

"OK."

Jack led his friends through his bedroom to his balcony. He opened the balcony doors.

It was getting dark.

"It's a really clear night, Dave," said Madeleine. "There are loads of stars. Oh, look ..."

"What can you see?" asked Dave.

"Someone is flashing a light from one of the boats on the sea."

"And someone is flashing back from the West Hill, from down by the caves," said Steve. "Let's go to the hill and see what's going on. We can tell Joy on the way."

"No, we can't. She's at a meeting for foster carers," said Madeleine.

"Oh, yes, I forgot. We won't be long anyway."

Chapter 9 The scruffy dog

Dave's mum and dad were walking up a path from the Old Town to the West Hill.

"I enjoyed that pint of beer with the tourists," Trevor said. "They were a friendly crowd, weren't they, Molly?"

"Yes, they were," said Dave's mum. "And they really enjoyed hearing about Macbeth ... Oh, look, there's Dave sitting on the hill with his friends."

Dave, Jack, Steve and Madeleine were sitting in the long grass on the slope above the path to the caves. Dave's mum and dad went to sit with them.

"Hi, everyone," said his mum. "It's very dark up here."

"Sssh," said Steve. "Look down there at the path to the caves. There, in the lamplight."

"What can you see?" asked Dave.

"There's a man walking along the path with a scruffy Jack Russell terrier. I think she's been in the sea. She's soaking wet."

"Can you see from here that it's a she?"

"Yes, I think so. She looks pregnant. Or maybe she's just fat. She's not very happy. Her tail is down between her legs ... I can't see anything now. They've gone down the steps to the caves."

"I think I know why we saw a light flashing," said Madeleine. "It's so difficult to get a mobile signal down in the Old Town. It's difficult on the fishing beach, too. Maybe the man with the dog couldn't get a signal down on the fishing beach. So he flashed his lamp to see if it was OK to come up to the caves. And then someone up here flashed back to say it was OK."

"Maybe," said Dave. "What did the man with the dog look like?"

"He was tall and thin, about thirty-five years old. He had short, fair hair. And he was wearing white shorts and a dark hoodie with a blue cotton scarf round his neck," said Jack.

"What colour was the dog?"

"White with black ears. And there was a big patch of black on its face. Why do you want to know?"

"For the same reason I always want to know. So that I can see what sighted people see."

"Joy will be back by now," said Steve. "Let's go home."

"OK," said Madeleine. "We can come back in the morning."

"Yes, let's all go home," said Dave's dad. "Oh, by the way, Jack – how did you phone Dave from your mobile this afternoon? It's not possible to get a signal in the caves."

"I wasn't in the caves. I phoned and then went in," said Jack.

"I didn't see you come in," said Dave's mum. "But maybe I was in the office getting souvenirs out of boxes."

"Ah, no," said Dave's dad. "I think Jack has his own secret entrance to the caves ... Hey, Jack, don't look so worried. I was only joking."

Chapter 10 So many dark places

The next morning, Steve and Madeleine were sitting together on the hill.

"There goes Dave, off to work," said Steve.

Dave was walking along the path to the caves with his dad. He was swinging his white stick in front of him. His dad couldn't guide him because his hands were full. He was carrying his Shakespeare costume in one hand and a big tin of biscuits for the Smugglers Adventure staff room in the other hand.

"Hi, Dave," shouted Madeleine. "It's me and Steve."

Dave turned and waved. "See you later, maybe," he shouted.

There was a loud yelp of a dog in pain.

"Oh, sorry," said Dave. He turned towards where the yelp had come from. "Did I hit your dog with my stick? I wasn't concentrating. Is it all right?"

"It's fine," a man grunted as he brushed past him. He was dragging a little dog along on a lead behind him.

"Were the man and the dog coming from the caves, Dad?" Dave asked quietly.

"Well, from that direction, yes."

"What was the man wearing?"

"Shorts and a hoodie. And a blue cotton scarf round his neck."

"It sounds like the man from last night. What kind of dog was it?"

"Well, it looked similar to the dog we saw last night. But it wasn't pregnant or fat."

"What colour was its fur?"

"Oh, white mostly. But its ears were black. And there was a patch of black on one side of its face. Anyway, it's time to open up," said Dave's dad. He took out his keys.

While Dave and his dad were letting themselves into the Smugglers Adventure, Steve and Madeleine were watching the man in the white shorts. He was dragging the little dog along the path from the caves.

"Isn't that the dog from last night?" said Steve.

"It looks a bit like it. But this one is much thinner."

"Maybe she's had her babies. She looks tired. Poor little thing. It's cruel."

"Mmm."

"Well, don't you think it's cruel, Madeleine?"

"Well, it is, yes."

"But it's only an animal, right?"

"Well …"

"Listen. She's whimpering. Shall we go and tell that man to stop dragging her along?"

"He looks scary to me, Steve."

"Yes, he does … My mum used to pull me along like that when she needed a fix of heroin. She used to drag me up and downstairs by my wrist. Why are you looking at me like that?"

"Oh, I just …"

"Yes, well, sorry if I've shocked you or upset you, Madeleine. I know your mum is dead – I mean, she is dead, isn't she? You don't think they'll find her one day?"

"No, I saw them kill her. I was on my way home from my friend's house. When I got near my house, there were lots of soldiers in the front garden. Dad and my brothers were lying on the ground. They were dead. The soldiers were kicking them to make sure they were all dead. And one of the soldiers was holding my mum's wrist. But he wasn't looking at my mum. He was looking down at my dad's body. So my mum was able to shake her head at me. She pointed down the road with her other hand. I knew I should keep walking. So I kept walking. Then I heard a shot. I turned around. Mum was on the ground and the soldiers were kicking her dead body. I kept walking until I got to the Chinhoyi Caves. Then I hid in the caves."

"Why did they kill your family?"

"Because my dad was in the opposition, against President Mugabe. Mugabe's soldiers often killed people from the opposition and their families."

"Do you miss your mum?"

"Of course I do. And my dad and my brothers."

"I don't miss my mum and dad ... Look, the dog is lying down now. Let's go down there."

Madeleine followed Steve down the steps that led to the path. The man was bending over the dog.

"Can we help?" Steve asked.

"No, I don't need any help," said the man. He picked the dog up. It lay limply in his arms and groaned.

"Has she had a Caesarean?" asked Steve. He pointed to a row of stitches on the dog's side.

"Yeah," said the man. He turned to walk down one of the paths leading to the Old Town and the fishing beach.

"Wait! Where are the puppies?" shouted Steve.

The man didn't answer. He walked quickly down the path.

"The puppies must be around here somewhere," said Steve. "Shall we follow the man or shall we look for the puppies?"

"Maybe we should look for the puppies. They could be in the caves. The man was going to the caves last night."

"Yes, but how would he have got into the caves?"

"Maybe someone let him in from the inside."

"But how would they have got in?"

"Well, maybe they hid when the caves shut yesterday. I mean, it's easy to hide in caves. There are so many dark places."

"But why would anyone want to hide in the caves and wait for someone to bring them a pregnant dog?"

"I don't know. Are Jack Russell puppies very expensive?"

"You could make about £2,000 if she had eight or nine puppies. If she's pure Jack Russell. Even if she's not, you could make quite a lot."

"Steve, those puppies must be somewhere."

"Right, I'll go and look for the puppies in the caves. You go down to the fishing beach and see if you can see their mum. The man was going in the direction of the fishing beach with her."

"I thought you didn't like the caves, Steve."

"This is different. We have to find the puppies. I'll go and get Jack. We'll go through the passageway from his cellar."

Chapter 11 Steve in the heart of darkness

As they made their way over Jack's patio and into the cellar, Steve told Jack about the newly-thin dog.

"OK, we'll look for the puppies," Jack said.

He climbed onto the box of firewood.

"We need to be quick. They could die," said Steve. He followed Jack backwards through the hole.

When they reached the opening, the briefcase was there again.

Jack shone his torch on it.

"I can hear footsteps," whispered Steve.

Jack switched off his torch.

There was a sound of chains jangling. Someone pulled the briefcase through the opening into the Smugglers Adventure.

"I bet there was money in that briefcase," said Steve. "Payment for the puppies. The man must have left them in the caves for someone to collect. Or maybe they're keeping them in the caves until they can sell them one by one."

Steve climbed through the opening. Jack followed him.

"Hello?" said Dave. He was standing near the smugglers' boat.

"Hi, Dave, it's us – Steve and Jack," said Steve. "Has anyone just walked past you?"

"Someone brushed past me just now."

"Was it a man or a woman?"

"I think it was a man. I could smell aftershave."

"Well, it's not important. Come on," said Steve.

As they made their way around the Smugglers Adventure, Jack told Dave about the dog. Steve shone Jack's torch into every corner they passed.

"There's no sign of the puppies anywhere," he said when they reached the souvenir shop.

Dave's dad looked up from the till as they came into the shop.

"Ah," he said. "You've been in the heart of darkness, Steve."

"What?"

"Heart of Darkness is a story by a writer called Joseph Conrad," said Dave's mum, coming into the souvenir shop. "Trevor means you don't mind being in the darkness of the caves any more."

"No, it's different now," said Steve. "Dave, will you look for the puppies when you're not busy?"

"OK."

"Thanks. We're going down to the fishing beach."

"Puppies?" said Dave's mum.

Chapter 12 Looking for the dog

When Steve and Jack reached the fishing beach, they saw Madeleine near the sea. She was leaning over the side of a boat. They ran down to join her.

The boat had a motor, but there was also a pair of oars lying across it. The name on the side of the boat was Sea Witch.

"There's an old coat on the floor of the boat," said Madeleine.

Steve reached down and felt under the coat. He felt something furry.

"I think you've found her, Madeleine," he said. "Maybe they were going to dump her at sea. But she's still warm. I think she's alive. Stand next to the boat, Jack. I'll pass her to you."

He got down onto the floor of the Sea Witch. He gently lifted the coat off the animal.

The little dog opened her eyes and whimpered as Steve picked her up. Her stomach was throbbing, but otherwise she was still.

Steve passed the dog to Jack and climbed out of the boat.

"Let's get her home to Joy," Steve said. He took the little dog from Jack and held her close to his own chest.

"Look who's coming," said Jack.

The man in the white shorts, hooded sweatshirt and blue scarf was walking towards them. He was carrying the briefcase with the blue cat sticker in his right hand.

He stopped in front of them.

"Where are you taking that dog?" he asked.

Steve didn't answer.

Sea Witch

"Give me the dog. I'll look after it," the man said. He leaned forward and pulled at the dog with his left hand. She yelped in pain.

Jack grabbed the man's left arm. Madeleine grabbed his right arm. They tried to pull him backwards. Steve walked as fast as he could up the beach. The dog was pushing her nose into his T-shirt. The man wrestled his way free from Jack and Madeleine. He started chasing Steve. But he tripped over a rope that was trailing from a fishing boat. He fell down. When he got up, a well-built fisherman was standing over him.

"I've been watching you, mate," said the fisherman. "Do you make a habit of chasing kids?"

"They've stolen my ..."

The man began to explain, but then changed his mind. He went back to the shore. He dropped the briefcase onto the floor of the Sea Witch. Then he started pushing the boat into the sea.

Chapter 13 The West Hill cliff lift

Madeleine, Jack and Steve walked along the promenade. The dog was whimpering and nuzzling Steve's stomach through his T-shirt.

They crossed the road and walked towards the cliff lift.

When they reached the lift entrance, Madeleine said to the man selling tickets, "We haven't got any money, and we need to get this dog home. She's dying."

The man waved them through.

"Thanks," said Steve.

"That's all right."

The man let them into the lift cabin. He shut and bolted the door. Steve sat down carefully. He held the dog close to him. A bell rang and the lift started to move up.

The dog stopped whimpering on the lift. But as they went up the steps onto the hill, she began again.

"At last," said Steve when they reached the front door of Joy's house.

Madeleine got out her key and let them in.

Joy came into the hall.

"Who's this?" she asked when she saw the dog in Steve's arms.

"She's had a Caesarean," said Steve. "And we don't know where the puppies are."

"Right, I'll make us all a cup of tea," said Joy. "I've got an old mug I can give the dog. I'll put some sugar in hers."

"Don't make hers too hot. Put plenty of milk in it," said Steve.

Chapter 14 The cavern

Dave had nearly finished his tour of the caves in search of the puppies. He had felt in every corner and opening he knew. He had hoped to feel something furry. But he had only felt the sandy rock of the caves.

He decided to check the chapel again. He had gone rather quickly through it because there had been a group of tourists looking round at the time.

When he returned, the tourists had gone. It was silent and still now in the chapel. Dave was sure he was alone. He walked close to the walls. He felt them carefully as he went. He felt the shape of the weird, flat statue. But there were no openings anywhere that could be a hiding place for puppies.

Dave decided to try the cavern where an elderly couple had lived from 1783 until 1786. He went to the bottom of the Monks' Walk. Then he clambered up the sandstone steps to the waxwork figures of the couple. He squeezed behind them to the back walls of the cavern. There were several alcoves in the walls of the cavern. He felt each alcove carefully.

He found an opening in one of the alcoves. He climbed through it. It led to another cavern. He decided to explore the cavern on his hands and knees. He didn't want to step on the newborn animals.

He started working his way around the walls of the cavern. At first, he could only feel the sandstone floor and walls. But then his hand touched something made of metal. He felt it with both hands. It was an old-fashioned weighing scale. There was a metal teaspoon on the floor beside it.

He left it where it was and crawled past it. Then he felt something on the cavern floor. It was something packed in a plastic sack.

Dave decided he needed to explore the cavern with his sighted friends.

So he felt his way out of the cavern and past the waxworks. He slithered down the steps and walked up the Monks' Walk to the ticket office.

His dad was standing behind the till at the ticket office.

"Hi, Dave," he said.

"Hi, Dad … Dad, is it OK if I go to Joy's house?"

"Yes, that's fine. We're not too busy at the moment. Can you go without a guide?"

"Yes. I'll use my stick."

"OK, but put your friends' numbers into my mobile before you go."

"Jack's, Madeleine's and Steve's? … OK."

Dave's dad handed him his mobile. Dave felt for the little bump on the 5 and keyed in his friends' numbers. He knew them by heart.

Chapter 15 Scruff

Joy brought a mug of warm tea over to Steve. She held it near the dog's nose.

The dog moved her head towards the mug. She began lapping up the tea.

"She's really thirsty," said Joy. "Madeleine, I've defrosted some prawns. They're on the table. See if the dog will eat them."

The dog pushed her head right down into the mug. She finished the tea. Then she turned her head back towards Steve's stomach. She closed her eyes.

Madeleine handed Steve some prawns.

Steve held a prawn under the dog's nose. She opened her eyes. She took the prawn from his hand. She bit it and swallowed it. She ate three more prawns. Then she closed her eyes again. She rested her chin on Steve's knee.

"That dog hasn't had a Caesarean," said Joy. "They wouldn't cut through the ribs to get to the womb. They would cut lower down. Look, the stitches are too high up."

Joy's mobile rang. She looked at it and said, "Oh, it's the fostering service. I'll talk to them upstairs."

Then the doorbell rang. Madeleine went to answer it. She came back into the kitchen with Dave.

He sat down at the table and told Madeleine, Jack and Steve about the hidden cavern.

"There was an old-fashioned weighing scale in there."

"Anything else?" asked Madeleine. She put Dave's right hand round the handle of a mug of tea.

"Thanks," he said. "There was a spoon. And something packed in a plastic sack. There was no sign of any puppies."

"Joy thinks the stitches are too high up for a Caesarean," said Jack.

"But you said the dog looked pregnant before."

"Yes, kind of fat, but not fat all over," said Steve.

Joy came into the kitchen.

"Hello, Dave," she said. "Help yourself to biscuits. They're on a plate just to the left of your left elbow."

"Thanks," said Dave.

He felt for the plate and took a biscuit.

"We'll need to ask a vet to take the dog's stitches out," said Joy.

"You mean, we're keeping Scruff?" asked Steve.

"Oh, so you've decided on a name," said Joy. "You really want to keep her, don't you, Steve? How do you feel about that, Madeleine?"

"It's OK with me," said Madeleine.

"Thanks," said Steve.

When Dave had finished his tea, he said, "Let's go down to the fishing beach. Maybe the puppies are there."

"OK," said Jack.

"I'll come, too," said Madeleine.

Steve gave them a beaming smile as they left.

"It's just you, me and Joy," he said to Scruff. He took a biscuit from the plate. Scruff raised her head. She sniffed the biscuity smell. Steve broke off a bit of biscuit. The dog took it gently from his hand.

Jack closed the front door behind him as Dave and Madeleine walked to the pavement.

Jack followed them and looked back at his own house next door.

Beth was standing at his dad's bedroom window. She was frowning as she looked down at Jack. Jack shivered.

Chapter 16 Another dog

Madeleine guided Dave around the boats on the fishing beach. Jack ran ahead to the shore. There was a strong wind. The waves crashed onto the sand and pebbles.

The Sea Witch was back on the beach near the water's edge. Every few seconds, a wave rushed in and hit the boat. Jack climbed into it and looked under the old coat on the floor, thinking he might find the puppies there. But there was nothing this time.

"Hey, what are you doing in my boat?" an angry voice shouted.

It was the man in the hooded sweatshirt and the blue scarf. He was leading a different dog behind him. It was a Jack Russell like Scruff, but this one had a patch of black fur on its back.

The man was looking at Jack. The dog was shaking. Its tail was down between its legs.

Jack got out of the boat.

"What's happening?" Dave asked Madeleine.

"The man who had Scruff is down on the beach with another dog. He's annoyed because Jack was in his boat," said Madeleine.

"What's happening now?" asked Dave.

"He's just picked up the dog and put it into the Sea Witch."

"The Sea Witch?"

"That's the name of the boat. He's pushing the boat into the sea," said Madeleine. "And now he's getting into it ..."

"Where's Jack?"

"He's walking back up the beach towards us."

"What's the man doing now?"

"He's just rowed out a bit and now he's put the oars down and ..."

"I can hear an engine. Has he just switched the engine on?"

"Yes. He's turning left in the direction of the East Hill."

"Maybe he's heading for Dover or Folkestone. The Channel ports."

"Maybe. But why?"

"I don't know ... The sea is very loud. It sounds rough out there."

"Yes, the waves are really high. There aren't any other boats out today."

Chapter 17 Huge waves

Jack stayed out for the rest of the day. He hated going home. Since Beth had moved in, it didn't feel like home any more.

When he finally went home in the evening, he ran straight upstairs to his room and stood on his balcony.

Jack looked down at the fishing beach. Huge waves were crashing onto the shore. The light of a small boat appeared round the headland of the East Hill. It moved towards the shore. Jack knew it wasn't a fishing boat. No fisherman would go out on such a rough sea.

The light on the boat began to flash. Once, twice, three times. There were three answering flashes from the West Hill. Then the boat and its light disappeared behind an enormous black wave.

Jack picked up his phone and called Steve.

"Sssh," whispered Steve. "Scruff is asleep on my lap. I can't talk now."

"OK, is Madeleine there?"

"She's gone to bed. Phone us in the morning, OK?"

"No, listen. Tell Madeleine I'll meet her at your house in the morning. We have to go down to the fishing beach."

"OK. I'll need to stay here with Scruff."

"Yes, I guessed that. And Dave will be working … OK, 'night Steve." Jack put the phone down.

His dad appeared at his bedroom door.

"Hi, Dad," said Jack. "Where's Beth?"

"She got a text from someone and went out."

Jack's dad sat on the chair at Jack's computer table. "How are you doing?" he asked.

Chapter 18 The wrecked boat

The sea was calmer the next morning. It was low tide when Jack and Madeleine reached the promenade near the fishing beach. Jack told Madeleine about the boat he had seen disappear the night before from his balcony.

"Have you told anyone else, Jack?" Madeleine asked as they walked around the empty fish stalls. There was nobody selling fish. None of the fishermen had been out in the night.

"Well, I told my dad. He said that I probably didn't see the boat come into shore because it was dark. But it wasn't that. The boat vanished while I was looking at the sea."

"Wow, you talked to your dad. He doesn't usually have time to talk to you these days."

"You're right. But he came into my bedroom last night. We talked for ages. Beth had gone out. And she didn't come back. She wasn't there at breakfast. It was great. Hey, Madeleine, look down there. What's going on?"

Madeleine looked down the beach. Some fishermen were standing around something. One of the fishermen left the group and came up the beach. He was trying to get a signal on his phone. He looked at Jack and Madeleine.

"I'm trying to get the coastguard," he said. "A boat has been washed up. There are bits of it everywhere. It was called the Sea Witch. What kind of crazy maniac would have taken a boat out last night?"

The fisherman went on walking up the beach.

"I know what kind of crazy maniac would have taken a boat out last night," said Jack.

"The man in the white shorts," said Madeleine. "Jack, what's that down there on the sand? It looks like a dog."

She pointed at a black and white shape at the water's edge. She started walking towards it. Jack followed her. He turned every so often to look at the group of fishermen on the other side of the beach. They were turning pieces of the wrecked boat over with their feet.

When Madeleine and Jack got down to the water's edge, they found a small black and white dog lying on its side on the wet sand.

"It's the dog the man took away in the Sea Witch," said Jack.

He touched the animal. "It's very cold," he said.

"But it's alive," said Madeleine. "Its stomach is moving. Look."

"Oh, yeah. Hey, look at those stitches, Madeleine. And it's got a really fat stomach. But this one can't be pregnant: it's a boy! Let's get him home quickly."

He unzipped his rain jacket and carefully picked the dog up. He placed him inside his jacket. Then he and Madeleine started walking up the beach.

Chapter 19 Brother and sister

"Another one?" said Steve as Jack sat down and opened his jacket to reveal the little dog.

Steve stood up and laid Scruff on an old blanket in a corner of the kitchen. He took the wet dog from Jack and sat down with him on the floor near Scruff.

"He'll die if we don't get him warm," Steve said.

"I'll make him some tea," said Madeleine. "And you go home and put some dry clothes on, Jack. You're soaked from carrying the wet dog."

"OK. I'll be back soon."

Jack went out to the hall. Scruff stood up unsteadily. She sniffed the air. Then she began to whimper. She put her front paws in Steve's lap, leaned over and licked the cold dog's wet nose. The dog slowly opened his eyes.

Madeleine brought a mug of tea and a hot water bottle. She put the mug on the floor. Then she slipped the hot water bottle under the blanket.

"That's a good idea," said Steve. He put the new dog on the blanket over the hot water bottle.

He and Madeleine looked down at the two little dogs. Scruff had curled herself round the new dog's wet body. She gently pushed his nose towards the mug of tea. The dog opened his eyes again, but he didn't move.

"I think they're brother and sister," said Steve.

"Of course they're brother and sister," said Madeleine. "Just like you and me."

"Yeah, well, I'll go and get an old towel to dry him," said Steve.

Chapter 20 Coventry Patmore

Back at home, Jack checked the pockets of his wet jeans to be sure he hadn't left anything in them. He found a folded piece of paper in one of the pockets. Then he remembered: it was the piece of paper which had fallen from Beth's pocket. He decided to look at it later. He didn't want Beth to see he had it. Jack put the piece of paper into the pocket of the clean jeans he had just put on. Then he took the wet clothes downstairs to put them in the washing machine.

When he got down to the hall, Beth was standing there. Her face was thick with make-up. There were bags under her eyes. She looked cross and tired, as if she hadn't slept all night.

"You're expecting me to wash a lot of clothes, Jack," she said.

"I'm not expecting you to wash them," said Jack.

He went to the kitchen. He pushed his clothes into the washing machine. Then he went back to Joy's house.

When he went into Joy's kitchen, Steve was putting a blanket over the dogs.

"What are you going to call the new dog?" Jack asked.

"I don't know. Any ideas?"

"Yes. Coventry Patmore."

"What did you say?"

"Coventry Patmore. He was a poet who lived in Hastings. Dave's dad dresses up as him sometimes. Coventry Patmore had a droopy moustache, a bit like the new dog's."

"But the new dog has got a beard, not a moustache," said Madeleine.

"He still looks like Coventry Patmore."

"Dave texted me while you were out," said Steve. "He wants you to meet him in the caves. He wants to show you the cavern he found yesterday. He said he texted you, but you didn't answer."

"Oh, my phone's on silent and I forgot to check it for messages," said Jack. "I'll text him now. What time shall we meet him, Madeleine?"

"After lunch," said Joy, coming into the kitchen. "I made vegetable soup before I went out this morning."

Then she saw the two dogs' heads peeping out from under the blanket.

"Steve," she said. "You've got two dogs now ..."

"Yes," said Steve. "Jack and Madeleine found Coventry Patmore and brought him home."

"You're calling the second dog after a dead poet?"

"Yes. Can I keep both dogs?" asked Steve.

"Well, we can't leave them out in this cold wet weather to die," said Joy. "They both look so weak."

Madeleine put four bowls of soup and some bread on the table. Steve put a bowl of soup beside the dogs.

"I'll have my soup later," said Joy. "I have to go to a foster carers' meeting. Bye, everyone."

Scruff stood up and shook off the blanket. She started to lap up the soup. Coventry Patmore staggered to his feet and joined Scruff at the soup bowl. Steve touched the row of stitches over the bulge in Coventry Patmore's stomach.

"It's OK, Coventry Patmore," he said. "We'll show Joy your stomach when she comes back. And then we'll take you to a vet."

Chapter 21 In the hidden cavern

Beth was out when Jack and Madeleine went to Jack's house.

Jack unlocked the cellar and put the key in his pocket. He didn't want Beth to lock them in when she came back.

He switched on his torch and they went to the back of the cellar. Jack climbed onto the box of firewood and squeezed his way backwards into the passageway. Madeleine followed him. They went down the passageway.

When they got to the opening, Jack shone his torch up and down the walls and said, "There's no briefcase here today."

They squeezed through the opening and made their way round the waxwork smugglers and the boat. Then they walked through the caves to the souvenir shop. Dave was standing at the entrance.

"Hi, Dave, it's us, Jack and Madeleine," said Jack.

"Hi," said Dave. "Follow me. I'll show you the cavern." Dave led Madeleine and Jack to the bottom of the Monks' Walk. They followed him up the steps to the waxworks of the elderly couple. Then he led them behind the waxworks and through the opening to the cavern.

It was totally dark inside. Dave heard a click as Jack switched his torch on.

"Can you see a weighing scale?" he asked.

"Yes," said Madeleine. "And a spoon. And a big plastic sack. Hang on, I'll tell you what's in it."

She went over to the sack and opened it.

"Oh, it's just lots of little plastic bags with zips at the top," she said.

Dave started to feel his way along the wall. "I went round the other way last time," he said. "Hey, you two, let's stick together!"

"We're behind you," said Jack.

"Good. Hang on. What's this?" Dave touched a large bookcase that was standing against the wall. "It feels like a bookcase, but these aren't books," he said, running his hand over lots of plastic packets on the shelves.

"No, they aren't books," said Jack. "They're packets of something. Dave, do you remember the drugs lessons we had in Year 8?"

"Yes."

"Well, the teachers showed us photos of packets of pure heroin mixed with sugar and stuff like that. The packets on the shelves look just like the packets in the photos."

"I think you might be right about the packets, Jack," said Madeleine. "There are lots of bags of sugar down here next to the bookcase, too."

"Let's sit on the floor and work out what's going on," said Jack.

They sat down in a row against the wall next to the bags of sugar.

"Turn your torch off. I can hear something," Dave whispered urgently.

Jack quickly switched his torch off.

They could hear clothes brushing against the sandstone. Someone was coming into the cavern. Then there was a click as the person switched on a torch.

Chapter 22 Bound and gagged

Madeleine and Jack could see the silhouette of a man near the cavern opening. The rest of the cavern was in darkness.

A second man appeared through the opening.

"Any news of Alan?" asked the first man.

"No. They have found many pieces of wood from the boat. But they have not found Alan," said the other man. He spoke with a French accent.

"And the dog?"

"No, they have not found the dog. So we have lost two dogs. One under the sea and one stolen by teenagers."

"The dog which drowned was carrying valuable cargo."

"Yes. At least the cargo was removed from the first dog before the teenagers stole her."

"Yes, that's one good thing."

"Mrs Skilling will have to choose someone to replace Alan. But that is not our problem. OK, I will count the packets into the sports bag. If the number is right, you will take the briefcase to the usual place."

The Frenchman walked over to the bookcase. He took a huge empty sports bag off his shoulder. The bag had a blue cat sticker on its side. The man began taking plastic packets from the shelves. He put them into the sports bag one by one. "Un, deux, trois, quatre …"

"This is taking too long," said the other man, impatiently. "It doesn't have to be the exact number."

"Yes, it does. Mrs Skilling expects us to be exact," said the Frenchman. "You know how she is … cinq, six, sept, huit … What is it? Why are you nudging me? Please stop interrupting me. I cannot count when you interrupt me."

"You can count later," said the Englishman. "Look what I've found." He shone his torch to the right of the bags of sugar.

The Frenchman stared at Jack, Dave and Madeleine.

The Englishman said to him, "Let's get as many packets as we can into the sports bag. Then we'll put the rest in that plastic sack over there. Thanks to these kids, we won't be able to use this place again. Don't move, kids. We've got knives and we'll use them if we need to. We can leave you here dead or alive. It's up to you."

The men were both wearing blue cotton scarves round their necks. They took them off. The Englishman tore his scarf in two. He tied one half round Jack's mouth and the other round Dave's. He secured them firmly with knots at the back of the boys' necks.

The Frenchman used his scarf to gag Madeleine. He said something in French as he struggled to tie a firm knot under her hair extensions.

Then the Frenchman bound their hands together behind their backs with chains. The chains were similar to the one attached to the briefcase. The Englishman used chains to tie their feet together.

Jack's torch had fallen on the ground. The Frenchman picked it up and put it in his own pocket.

Chapter 23 At the vet's

When Joy came in from her meeting, Steve was cuddling Coventry Patmore on his lap. Scruff was walking round the kitchen.

"Aren't Madeleine and Jack back yet?" asked Joy.

"No."

"You look worried, love," said Joy.

"Coventry Patmore vomited up his soup," said Steve.

"Oh, dear. Let me look at him." Joy went over to Steve and stroked the dog. She gently touched the line of stitches in the dog's stomach.

"Steve, why didn't you tell me about this?" she asked.

"There wasn't time," said Steve.

"Look, I don't know what's going on, but we need to take this dog to a vet," said Joy.

"I know," said Steve. "But where will we get the money to pay the vet's bill?"

"I'm not sure, love, but we have no choice. And we'd better take Scruff as well. We'll find out when her stitches need to come out. I'll get the phone book. We'll see if we can find a vet who'll see us today."

Joy phoned several vets. Finally she found one who agreed to see Scruff and Coventry Patmore immediately. Joy phoned for a cab.

When the cab arrived, Joy carried Scruff into it. Steve followed her, carrying Coventry Patmore.

When they got to the vet's surgery, the vet was waiting for them.

"Hi, I'm Trish," she said. "OK, I'll look at this one first." She pointed at Scruff. "Put her on the table."

Joy held Scruff on the table. Trish felt her stomach.

"What's her name?" asked Trish.

"Scruff," said Steve.

"When do her stitches need to come out?" asked Joy.

"They don't need to come out. They're soluble," said Trish. "You just need to keep them clean. My nurse, Natalie, will clean the area around them."

The vet looked over at a girl in a white coat. The girl had thin lips that were painted bright red. She was getting her phone out of her pocket.

"Natalie, put that away," said Trish. "Would you clean Scruff's stitches, please?"

Natalie picked Scruff up and took her to another table. Scruff started whimpering and struggling.

"Have you got long nails?" Steve asked Natalie.

"No, they're short. Why?" Natalie asked.

"Scruff is frightened of you," said Steve. "I thought maybe your nails were digging into her."

"Well, they're not."

The vet frowned. Then she said, "OK, let's have a look at the other dog."

"His name is Coventry Patmore," said Steve. He put the dog on the table.

"Patmore … Ah, you named him after a poet." The vet gently stroked the bulging stomach.

"Who did this to him?" she asked. She was staring at the stitches, looking concerned.

"I don't know."

"He's not your dog?"

"Well, he is now. We rescued him."

"Ah. Oh dear, excuse me a moment."

The vet left Steve holding Coventry Patmore on the table. She strode over to Natalie. Natalie was holding Scruff with one hand and taking out her phone again with the other.

"Natalie! This is very unprofessional. What do you think you're doing? Put your phone away," said the vet.

The vet went back to Steve.

"I'll need to operate on Coventry Patmore," she said. "When did he last have anything to eat or drink?"

"Well, he had a few sips of soup at lunchtime, but he vomited it up," said Steve.

"Will the operation be expensive?" asked Joy.

"It won't be cheap. But if I don't operate, this dog will die," said the vet. "And we need to find out exactly what that is." She pointed to the bulge in Coventry Patmore's stomach. "I think we'll need to call the police."

Scruff suddenly jumped onto the floor. Coventry Patmore wriggled under Steve's hands.

Scruff ran to the window. Then she ran to the door and then back to the window. She jumped at the glass.

"The police?" said Steve.

Scruff started running round the room in circles.

Trish took a dog treat from a packet on a shelf.

Scruff stopped running and came over to eat the treat.

"I'd better get in touch with the police so I can start operating," said Trish.

"She's off again," said Joy. "She runs whenever anyone says the word 'police'."

Scruff was running in circles again. Trish grabbed her. She held her close and stroked her.

Steve's mobile rang. Steve held Coventry Patmore close to his chest with his left arm as he took his phone out of his pocket with his right hand.

"Hi Trevor," he said. "No, they were going to meet Dave in the caves. Are you sure they're not there? ... Trevor, try going behind the waxworks of the old couple at the bottom of the Monks' Walk ... Yes, Dave found a hidden cavern there ... Yes, he texted me to tell me ... OK, bye."

Natalie stared at Steve. When he had put his mobile back in his pocket, she asked, "Who were you talking to about the Monks' Walk?"

"Oh, nobody," Steve lied.

"Can I go now?" Natalie asked Trish.

"I suppose so," said Trish.

When Natalie had left, the vet said, "She's a strange girl. She's a very skilled nurse but ..."

"But?" Joy asked.

"Oh, I don't know. A few things have disappeared recently – some anaesthetic and some surgical instruments have gone. And Natalie is the only person apart from me who has a key to the cupboards in this room. And Scruff was terrified of her."

"Oh, dear," said Joy. "What a worry for you. Steve looks worried, too."

"Yes, I am," said Steve. "When Dave's dad phoned, he sounded anxious about Dave, Madeleine and Jack. I think something is going on at the caves, but I don't know what."

Chapter 24 In the darkness

After emptying the shelves, the Englishman and the Frenchman had left the cavern. They had taken the plastic sack and sports bag full of packets with them.

Madeleine, Jack and Dave were left in the dark, trying to get free.

The chains dug into their hands and feet every time they tried to move. And the gags were very uncomfortable.

Dave thought he could get across to the opening on his side. He was used to feeling his way around. But it wouldn't be easy with his hands tied behind his back. He would use his elbows, knees and hips.

Back at the souvenir shop, Molly was putting packets of Hastings Fudge on the shelves when the men passed by. She watched them as they pushed open the exit gate. She had seen them when they had come in earlier. They hadn't been carrying the huge plastic sack. And the sports bag had been empty. Molly wondered if they had stolen something from the caves.

The two men walked quickly along the path from the caves. Trevor was coming towards them. They elbowed him out of their way. Then they disappeared down one of the paths that led to the Old Town.

The men made Trevor feel very uneasy. He hurried along the path to the Smugglers Adventure where he met Molly coming out.

"I'm going to follow those men," said Molly.

"OK," said Trevor. "I'm going to see if Dave is OK. Be careful."

He walked through the caves, but there was no sign of Dave.

Trevor went to the souvenir shop and picked up the phone behind the counter. First he phoned Dave's mobile, but there was no answer. So he phoned Steve.

When Steve told him that Dave had found a hidden cavern behind the waxworks of the elderly couple, Trevor ran all the way down the Monks' Walk. He clambered up the steps. Then he edged his way round behind the waxworks. He started looking for a hidden entrance to a cavern.

He heard a muffled sound from behind the cave wall.

"Is anyone there?" he shouted.

There was a loud groan.

Trevor moved along the cave wall to where the groan had come from. He felt an opening and pushed his way through it.

There was a strangled moan as he accidentally kicked Dave in the dark.

Trevor knelt down. He put his hand out in the darkness. He felt his son's short hair and sticky-out fringe.

"Dave!" he said.

Dave groaned again. He had made his way towards the opening on his side.

Trevor touched his son's face and felt the gag. "OK, just keep still," he said. "I didn't bring a torch."

When Trevor had untied the gag, Dave coughed and said, "Feel behind my back and untie the chain around my wrists."

When Trevor had freed Dave's hands, Dave untied the chain around his feet.

"Wait here, Dad," he said as he started to feel his way back along the wall and around the bookcase to his friends.

It took Dave some time to untie the gags and the chains around Madeleine's and Jack's wrists. When they were off, Madeleine and Jack coughed as they undid the chains from their feet.

They stood up and stretched their arms.

"Now, keep close to me. We'll feel our way back to Dad," said Dave. "All right, Dad?" he called into the darkness.

"Yes, I'm still here."

They made their way through the darkness to Dave's dad. Then they squeezed through the opening into the dim light around the waxwork couple.

"Let's go up the Monks' Walk to the entrance. I'll phone the police from there," said Trevor. "You three go home and get something to eat and drink."

"Yes, come to my house," said Jack.

When they reached the entrance to the caves, Dave's dad picked up the phone.

Dave pulled something out from under his jumper. "What shall I do with this? I felt it on the floor of the cavern. I decided to pick it up and bring it with me."

It was the small briefcase with the cat sticker on it.

"Give it to the police?" said Madeleine.

"OK." Dave took his rucksack from behind the counter and pushed the briefcase into it.

His dad put the phone down. "I saw a blue cat sticker on the briefcase," he said. "One of the men was carrying a sports bag with a blue cat sticker on it ... Anyway, the police said they'll send someone over to check out the cavern. And then they'll go to your house, Jack. And then to yours, Madeleine. They need to talk to you three."

Chapter 25 Did I scare you?

When they reached his house, Jack opened the front door and went into the hall. Madeleine and Dave followed him. They could hear the TV in the living room. The unlocked padlock was hanging off the living room door.

"Let's get some food," said Jack.

There were some plastic Indian takeaway boxes on the kitchen table.

"Cool," said Jack. "Dad's bought a takeaway."

Beth came into the kitchen and opened the fridge. She took out a chilled bottle of white wine.

"Good evening," she said.

Jack ignored her and said, "Madeleine, take what you want. Here's a plate. Dave, do you like lamb korma? Or do you want vegetable biryani?"

"I like both," said Dave.

Jack and Madeleine spooned food onto three plates.

Beth left the kitchen. She was carrying the bottle of wine and two glasses.

"Let's eat this in the living room," said Jack. "I haven't watched TV for ages. I'll carry your plate, Dave. And I'll come back and get some drinks for us."

Madeleine took Dave's arm, and they went into the hall.

Jack opened the living room door and led his friends in.

"Hi, Dad," he said.

"Hi," said his dad, who was sitting on the sofa next to Beth. "I'm glad your friends are here. I bought loads of food."

Beth frowned. She handed Jack's dad a glass of wine.

Madeleine guided Dave to one of the two armchairs in the room. Then she sat on the other one with her plate of vegetable biryani.

Dave put his rucksack next to the armchair. The small briefcase was still inside.

Jack took Dave's plate of food to him.

"Here you are, Dave," he said. "There's korma at twelve o'clock and biryani at six o'clock on your plate."

Dave took the plate. Jack put the handle of a fork into Dave's right hand. Then he went over to the sofa. He sat down on the floor near his dad and began eating his plate of Indian food.

"Cheers!" said Beth, raising her glass of wine to clink glasses with Jack's dad.

"Sssh," said Jack's dad. He pointed at the television screen. "Look. Hastings beach. A body has been washed up."

"A wrecked boat was discovered on the fishing beach yesterday," a TV reporter's voice was saying. "And now police are trying to identify the body of a man wearing white shorts, a hooded top and a blue cotton scarf. The body was found washed up on the shore at Hastings this morning."

Beth put her glass down on the floor. She picked up her handbag, took out a tissue and blew her nose.

Then she said, "Where's the remote?"

Jack's dad handed her the remote control and she turned the television off.

"I don't like sad news," she said. "Let's talk about happier things ...What are you staring at, Jack?"

Jack turned away without answering. He went over to Dave.

"Finished?" he asked.

"Er … Well, I've nearly finished," said Dave as Jack took his plate.

"I can't eat any more," lied Madeleine. "Come on, Dave. Let's wash our plates up." She went over to Dave.

Dave put his rucksack on his back and took Madeleine's arm. They followed Jack into the kitchen.

"What were you staring at in there?" Madeleine asked Jack.

"Beth's bag," said Jack. "Didn't you see the cat sticker on it? It was the same as the ones on the briefcase and the sports bag. Dave, make sure you keep the briefcase hidden."

"So Beth has got something to do with all this," said Madeleine. "Let's go to my house. We can talk freely there."

As Madeleine took Dave's arm to guide him into the hall, Dave said, "Coming, Jack?"

"Yes, I'll come when I've washed the plates up."

He heard the front door bang shut after them. He turned the tap on and began washing the plates.

Beth came quietly into the kitchen. She tapped Jack on the shoulder.

He jumped and turned around. Beth was holding her handbag.

"What is it, Jack?" she asked. "Did I scare you?"

"No. I just didn't hear you coming into the kitchen. Are you going out? You've got your coat on."

"Yes, I just need to get a few things from my flat. And your dad is going out soon – he's meeting some of his friends at the pub for a pint."

"Is he?"

"Yes. I see your friends have gone. Now that they've eaten our dinner."

Jack said nothing.

"That blind boy seems to be very fond of his rucksack," Beth said.

Jack ignored her. He finished washing the plates. Then he turned around.

"Are you staying at home this evening, Jack?" Beth asked. She was frowning and looking straight into his eyes.

"Yes," he lied, staring back into her eyes.

"Good." Her face relaxed. "I'll see you later."

When she had left the house, Jack went into the living room.

His dad looked up and smiled.

"Dad, don't go out tonight," Jack said.

"No, I don't think I will. I'm really tired. I'll phone and cancel. How did you know I was going out?"

"Beth told me."

"Yes, that was when I thought she would be here all evening. But now that you and I have got the house to ourselves, I would rather stay in."

"Dad, why do you let her take over?"

"It just happened."

"Dad, she's bad."

"How do you mean?"

"Well, I don't know what she wants from you. I don't know if she wants to marry you, or if she wants this house. But she's mixed up in something bad, Dad."

"What kind of thing?"

"Dad, can we go next door and talk there? The others are waiting for me. Please, Dad."

"Well, if you think it will be all right with Joy … OK, just for a while. Oh, and before I forget, I wanted to give you your pocket money, Jack. Here you are."

He handed Jack a £20 note. Jack pushed the money into his jeans pocket. As he did so, he felt the piece of folded paper that had fallen from Beth's dress pocket. He took it out and unfolded it.

"What's that?" his dad asked.

"Oh, Beth dropped it and I picked it up," said Jack.

His dad looked over his shoulder and read the sheet of paper. Then he hugged Jack.

"Jack, this is wonderful."

"Hang on, what's wonderful? It's just a ..."

"A pregnancy test result. Beth isn't pregnant!"

"You mean, you thought she was?"

"She told me she was. That's why I couldn't ask her to leave. But she isn't! Look! It's negative."

"And she let you think it was positive?"

"Yes. First she told me she thought she was pregnant. Then she said she had had a test done and it was positive. But look, here's her name, oh, and our address, and ... well, look – it's negative!"

"So that's the hold she had over you," said Jack.

"Come on, let's go to Joy's house," said his dad.

Chapter 26 The P-word

As Madeleine opened the front door to Jack and his dad, a cab stopped outside the house.

Joy and Steve got out of the cab. They followed Madeleine and Jack into the house. Steve was carrying Scruff in his arms.

"Come into the kitchen, everyone," said Joy.

"I've cooked spaghetti for you," Madeleine said to Joy and Steve. "The rest of us had an Indian takeaway at Jack's house."

"Great. Thanks. I'm really hungry," said Joy. She went over to the kitchen sink and washed her hands.

"Where's Coventry Patmore?" asked Madeleine.

"Who's Coventry Patmore?" asked Jack's dad, confused.

"A dog," said Madeleine. "Scruff's brother."

"We left him at the vet's," said Joy.

"The vet is going to operate on Coventry Patmore," said Steve. "She's going to open his stomach."

"I don't know what's going on," said Jack's dad. He sat down at the kitchen table beside Joy. "Jack, you said you've got things to tell me."

"Dad, we haven't got much time to talk. Dave's dad called the police. They're going to come and talk to us."

"The police?" Jack's dad said.

Scruff had been staring at the spaghetti on the table. But she suddenly jumped off Steve's lap. She started running around the kitchen. She jumped at the door every time she passed it.

"Why's she running around the kitchen?" asked Jack's dad.

“Because you said P-O-L-I-C-E,” said Steve between mouthfuls of spaghetti. “I think they trained the dogs to run when they hear that word. I think they put the stuff in dogs’ stomachs because dogs can run away. Suitcases can’t run away.”

“What do you mean?” asked Jack’s dad. “What stuff?”

They were interrupted by the doorbell. Steve stood up. He grabbed hold of Scruff. Madeleine went to answer the door.

She came back with a man and a woman. They were both wearing jeans and sweatshirts. They were holding police ID cards in their hands.

“OK,” said Joy. “Sit down. Just don’t say the word P-O-L-I-C-E.”

“OK, but why not? That’s what we are. We’re, er … P-O-L-I-C-E.”

“The dog goes crazy when anyone says it. We think she’s been trained to run away as fast as she can when she hears the word.”

“You’re not in uniform,” said Madeleine.

“No, and we came in an unmarked car,” said the woman. “It’ll be safer for you if nobody knows we’re here. And you’d better keep the dog hidden.”

“Safer?” said Jack’s dad.

“There’s another dog. Scruff’s brother,” interrupted Steve. “He’s at the vet’s.”

“Yes, we had a phone call from the vet,” said the policeman. “She wants police officers with her during the operation on the other dog.”

Scruff ran at the door. Then she started running round in circles. Steve grabbed her and held her still.

"She wants police officers with her during the operation?" repeated Jack's dad.

Scruff struggled in Steve's arms.

"Please stop saying the P-word, everyone," said Joy.

"Sorry," said the policeman and Jack's dad at the same time.

"Right, we'll take written statements later," said the policewoman. "But for now, just tell me everything that's happened."

Steve told her about the man in the white shorts. And he told her that Scruff had gone into the caves fat and come out thin. Then he told her they had found Scruff in the boat and brought her home. Then Jack told her they had found Coventry Patmore on the sand while the fishermen were examining the broken boat on the shore.

"So probably the man in the white shorts was trying to sail to the fishing beach with Coventry Patmore on the night of the storm. And the dog made it to the beach, but the man didn't. Did you know that a man's body was found on the shore?"

"Yes, we saw it on the news," said Jack. "I think that was when Beth suddenly decided to go out."

"Beth?"

"Beth is a horrible woman. She moved in with us when my mum died," said Jack. "She's crazy about my dad. Anyway, we were watching the news. She wanted us to switch it off after the bit about the man's body. That was when I noticed the cat sticker on her bag."

"What cat sticker?"

"There is the same cat sticker on the sports bag and briefcase."

"What sports bag and briefcase?" asked Jack's dad.

"Here's the briefcase," said Dave. He pulled it out of his rucksack.

The policeman reached over the table and took it from him.

"It's locked," he said. "I wonder why it's got this chain hanging from it. It's like the chains they tied you up with. Your dad gave them to us, Dave."

"Tied them up with?" asked Jack's dad.

"Yes, this afternoon," said Jack. "Madeleine and I met Dave. We wanted to look at a hidden cavern he had found. The men caught us in the cavern. They tied us up with chains. And they gagged us with their scarves. All the men involved in this thing wore blue scarves. Maybe it's a kind of uniform. A secret sign like the blue cat stickers. Oh, I forgot to put the cellar door key back. I forgot to lock it, too."

He took the key out of his pocket.

"What's the connection with the cellar?"

"There's a passageway from the back of our cellar to the caves. We've been using it most days. And this briefcase was often at the end of the passageway."

"This briefcase ...," said the policewoman. "Let's look inside it."

She took a wallet of small tools out of her shoulder bag. She opened the briefcase with a tool that looked like a small screwdriver.

There were piles of £20 and €50 notes inside the briefcase. Each pile was held together with rubber bands. There was also a notebook.

The policewoman opened the notebook. She showed everyone the pages inside. Each page was divided into columns: DATE, TIME, AMOUNT, PAID BY and PAID TO.

And each column had been filled in. The PAID BY and PAID TO columns were filled in with initials.

While they were still looking at the notebook, the policeman said, "I think we need to talk to Beth. What's her surname?"

"Skilling," said Jack's dad.

"Skilling?" said Dave. "The two men who tied us up were talking about a Mrs Skilling. I think she was their boss."

"Is she coming back to your house tonight, sir?" the policeman asked Jack's dad.

"Probably," groaned Jack.

"Right, we'll have someone waiting for her. But we'll visit her at home as well. Can you give us her address?"

"Somewhere on the seafront," said Jack's dad. "I've never been there."

"Well, if Beth Skilling is her real name, we'll find her address," said the policewoman. "I'll just get that organized."

While the policewoman was talking into her mobile, the policeman said, "Dave, your dad told us everything he knew. And we saw the cavern. But could you tell us what happened in your own words?"

Chapter 27 Molly keeps watch

Molly was sitting outside a café near the fishing beach. There was a pot of tea and a cup and saucer in front of her. She had followed the two men and watched them go into a building next door to the café.

After a while, a young woman stopped in front of the building. Her thin lips were painted bright red. She tried to open the front door with a key, but it wouldn't open, so she rang the bell. One of the men opened the door and let her in. Probably the door had been bolted on the inside.

Molly poured herself a cup of tea. She took a sip.

Her mobile vibrated. It was a text from Trevor.

"Where are you?" she read.

"At the café near Webbe's," she texted back. "The men are in the building next to the café. Is Dave with you?"

"He is at Joy or Jack's house," Trevor texted. "Will tell the police where you are."

"Police?" Molly texted back.

A woman walked past her table. Molly recognized her. It was the woman who had moved in with Jack's dad. Molly tried to remember her name. Beth?! Yes, that was it. Beth.

Beth was getting a key out of her handbag. Molly saw that there was a cat sticker on the bag. It looked like the same sticker she had seen on the man's sports bag.

Beth tried to open the front door, but it didn't open. She rang the bell. The girl with thin red lips opened the door and let her in.

Molly texted Trevor again.

"Beth went into the building."

She drank her tea and then her mobile rang. It was a call from Trevor.

"Molly, stay there. This is serious. The police are on their way. Are you OK?"

"Yes, I don't think Beth saw me. I don't think she knows who I am."

"OK, look, I have to go now. I'm going to Joy's house. Dave is there."

"OK. I'll stay here."

Chapter 28 Police protection

"Thank you all," said the policewoman. "We'll take official statements later."

The doorbell rang. Madeleine opened the door. Trish, the vet, was standing there. Coventry Patmore was asleep in her arms.

"Come in," said Madeleine. "Everyone is in the kitchen. We've just told the P-O-L-I-C-E everything."

Trish followed her into the kitchen.

"Coventry Patmore!" said Steve. He put Scruff on the floor and went over to Trish. "Is he all right?"

"He's OK, but don't give him any rich food for the next few days. Can I put him on that blanket down there?"

"Sure."

Trish gently laid the dog on the blanket. Scruff immediately walked over and lay curled around him. She licked his back.

"He's very thin now," said Steve. "What did you find when you operated?"

"Bags of white powder. The officers who stayed with me while I operated drove me here. Then they took the powder away for analysis. They think it's pure heroin. I suspected something like that. That's why I needed the officers with me. I needed their protection. But I also needed them as witnesses. I didn't want to be accused of heroin smuggling."

"Why would anyone accuse you?"

"Well, the ... you know ... P-O-L-I-C-E will want to find out who sewed the bags into the dogs' stomachs. Only a vet could do that. And only a vet would have the equipment to do it. Only a vet or ..."

"Or …?"

"Or a veterinary nurse. A veterinary nurse sees operations every day. Natalie would know exactly what to do."

"Do you think Natalie operated on the dogs and stitched the drugs into their stomachs?"

"It's possible …"

The doorbell rang. Madeleine went to the door. It was Dave's dad.

"Hi," he said. "Is Dave here?"

"Yes. The police are here, too."

Dave's dad followed Madeleine to the kitchen.

"Are you all OK?" he asked.

"We're fine," they all said together.

The policeman's mobile rang. He went into the hall. They heard him talking quietly. Then they heard him shout, "Why didn't you arrest her with the others?"

When he came back into the kitchen, he said, "They've found the veterinary nurse. And they've found the men who tied you three up. They've also found the woman who is probably the mastermind behind the heroin smuggling operation."

"Who didn't they arrest?" asked Jack.

"The woman who is probably the mastermind," said the policeman.

Chapter 29 She won't be back

Madeleine and Joy were washing up.

"Are you all right after all that happened in the cavern, love?" Joy asked.

"I've had worse experiences than that," Madeleine said.

Jack was sitting at the table with his dad. Steve was on the floor. He was stroking Scruff. Scruff was awake, but she was still curled around the sleeping Coventry Patmore.

"What do you want to do now, Jack?" his dad asked.

"I want to go home. I want to sit on the sofa and watch TV like I did when Mum was alive."

"Right, let's go and sit on our sofa then."

"And if Beth comes back, you won't let her in. Not even if the police want you to."

"No, I promise I won't. But she won't be back anyway. Oh, Jack, how could I have been so stupid?"

"You were upset about Mum. I suppose you didn't know what you were doing. And then Beth told you she was pregnant. But that was a lie. Dad, you're free of her now. Come on, let's go home. Actually, let's all go. Let's all go and sit in our living room."

"OK, we'll all go," said Jack's dad.

Joy came back from the kitchen with big wet patches of washing-up water on her sweatshirt. "Yes, let's all go to your house and watch TV, Jack. Steve, you and I will carry a dog each. We'll take one of their blankets, too."

As they left the house, Madeleine saw an envelope on the floor near the front door. She picked it up.

Chapter 30 Tonight's top story

Joy and Steve laid the dogs on their blanket in the living room at Jack's house. Madeleine handed Joy the envelope she had picked up.

"Thanks," said Joy. "Oh, it was delivered by hand." She tore open the envelope and took out a printed sheet of paper and a cheque.

"It's from Social Services. One of the fostering team probably dropped it in," she said. "Oh, they've paid me for …"

"For what?" asked Steve.

"Um … Steve, you know when I was out at meetings? Well, I was helping a boy. They had wanted me to foster him. I said I couldn't. But I agreed to talk to him and listen to him. I didn't tell you because I thought you would be jealous."

"Don't worry," said Steve. "It's fine with me. Oh, Coventry Patmore just opened one eye. Oh, he's shut it again."

"I'll be able to pay the vet's bill with this money," said Joy.

"That's great," said Jack, who was sitting on the sofa beside his dad. "Right, let's see what's on TV. I'll try BBC1 first." He picked up the remote control.

"It'll only be the news at this time," said Steve. "Yes, look, the local news has just started."

"And now for our top story tonight," the woman in the studio was saying. "Police have raided a flat opposite the fishing beach in Hastings. We'll go straight to our reporter,

John Davies. John is reporting live from Hastings fishing beach … Over to you, John …"

"Yes, Joanna, the police have arrested some alleged drug traffickers here in Hastings. The arrests took place at a flat across the road from here. The suspects were handcuffed and driven away around an hour ago. For the moment, the police aren't giving out too much information, but it seems the case involves large quantities of heroin. We'll keep you updated as soon as we know anything more, Joanna."

Jack picked up the remote control and pressed standby.

"I'm trying to understand it all," Jack's dad said. "You know, Beth and the cat sticker connection. I mean, what was her role in all this?"

"The two men who tied us up talked about her as if she was their boss," said Jack. "The Frenchman said Mrs Skilling expected them to be exact. That was when he was counting the packets."

"Maybe she gave the orders," said Joy. "The policeman told us they had found the woman who is probably the mastermind behind the heroin smuggling operation. It must have been Beth Skilling."

"Pure heroin would probably be delivered to the gang's headquarters on the French coast. Then someone would take Natalie to France with a dog. She would have the vet's supplies she had stolen from Trish with her, too. Natalie would sew the packs of pure heroin into the dog's stomach in France," Steve said.

"And then they would travel back from France to England through the Eurotunnel. The Eurotunnel port at Folkestone is only about thirty-five miles from Hastings," said Joy. "They probably drove dogs from the French coast to Folkestone and on to Hastings quite often."

"Apart from last time, when the man brought Coventry Patmore to Hastings by boat," said Jack.

"Yes, apart from last time," said Joy. "Anyway, once they were in Hastings, Beth would probably send a man up to the caves. He would signal to the man down at the fishing beach. Then the other man would know that it was OK to come up with the dog. And then Beth would tell Natalie to join the men in the caves. Natalie would remove the pure heroin from the dog's stomach in the hidden cavern at the end of the Monks' Walk."

"And then one of the men would take the dog either back to Natalie's flat or straight back to France. It would depend on when they expected the next delivery at their headquarters," said Joy.

"Yes, probably Beth would tell Natalie and the men when a new delivery of pure heroin was going to arrive in France," said Madeleine.

"But why did they need the briefcase?" said Joy.

"Well, that was probably how each person collected their money," said Madeleine. "Beth would have organized the payments. She probably gave one of the men money to put in the briefcase. And he would leave it in the opening behind the boat. And then Beth would tell each person when to collect their cash."

"So Beth's role was to give orders. And she probably took a lot of money for herself."

"Well, yes, she probably gave the orders," said Madeleine. "But she also dealt with things when they went wrong. She had to find a replacement for the man who drowned. That's what I understood when the men were talking in the cavern."

"She probably didn't take money for herself – her money would come in later."

"You mean, she would get her money when people started selling the heroin on the streets."

"Yes. She would make millions of pounds then."

"I was crazy to let Beth anywhere near us," said Jack's dad. "I wonder what she wanted from me. Do you think she wanted our house with its passageway to the caves?"

"No, she didn't know about that," said Jack.

"She wanted you. She was mad about you," Joy said to Jack's dad. "Even wicked people like Beth fall in love. She wanted to make you hers."

Jack's dad shivered. Then he said, "I'll get some drinks."

As he stood up to go to the kitchen, the doorbell rang. He opened the front door. Molly and Trevor were standing there.

"Is Dave with you?" Molly asked.

"Yes, he's in the living room. You two go in and I'll bring some drinks," said Jack's dad.

"Great," said Molly. "And tomorrow evening you must all come to our house."

Chapter 31 Here's to all four of you

The next morning, Jack, Madeleine and Dave went to the police station to give their statements. Madeleine looked after the dogs in the afternoon, so that Steve could go to the police station to give his statement. In the evening, she took the dogs to Dave's house.

When Steve finally arrived at Dave's house, everyone else was there. The dogs' tails wagged frantically when Steve walked into the living room.

Dave pressed a button on the top of a clock on the mantelpiece.

"It's 10.21 pm," a robot voice said from the clock.

"The news will be on now if you want," said Dave.

"There might be something about the dogs," said Steve as Trevor pressed the remote control.

"So we now go over to our reporter John Davies in Hastings for the latest on the multi-million pound drugs raid that took place there yesterday," the man in the studio was saying.

"Well, Jeremy," said the reporter. "I'm standing here on the fishing beach on this lovely calm evening. The building where the police raid took place yesterday is over on the other side of the road."

Steve and Joy held the dogs close to them after the reporter said the word "police".

"Do we know any more about the drugs trafficking operation, John?" asked Jeremy in the studio.

"Well, it could have resulted in heroin worth millions of pounds flooding our streets. But the gang was caught before they were able to start selling the stuff."

"What about the contact on the continent? Have they arrested him?"

"One of the men arrested was a French citizen. He came over here regularly. One of his roles was to help mix the heroin and weigh it into small bags ready for the street."

"And where did they do the weighing and packaging? In the flat that was raided?"

"No, they normally did the weighing and packaging in a hidden cavern in the Smugglers Adventure tourist attraction in the caves in the West Hill. But their hiding place was discovered. So they moved everything to the fishing beach flat."

"And whose flat was it? Were the men renting it?"

"No, the owner of the flat is Natalie Stewart, a veterinary nurse. She was arrested yesterday, too. Ms Stewart and her fellow-traffickers regularly drove to and from the Continent through the Eurotunnel with a small dog in the car. The gang's man in France would give Ms Stewart a bag of pure heroin and she would sew the drugs into the stomach of the animal. Then she would be driven back to England with the dog. They would drive the dog to Hastings and take it to the hidden cavern at the Smugglers Adventure. It's very dark and lonely on the West Hill at night. So it was the ideal place for their criminal activities. Unlike the flat – the flat is in an area with plenty of nightlife. Anyway, the flat would have been too small for the operation because it was full of other dogs."

Joanna and Jeremy in the studio came back on the screen.

"Other dogs?" said Joanna.

"Yes, I'll come to that ..."

"But didn't the staff at border control ever notice a dog in the car?" interrupted Joanna.

"Well, Joanna, no, they didn't see the dog till the last trip. The dog would have been hidden under a coat or rug or something. However, the nurse wasn't in the car with the dog on the last trip back to England. She had stayed in the gang's headquarters near Calais to operate on another animal. An official became suspicious when he thought he heard a dog whining in the car. He asked the driver to open the car door. The man opened it and shouted 'police', at which point the dog jumped out of the car and ran like the wind. The man was arrested for attempting to bring a dog into the country without a passport or microchip. When the police questioned him, he refused to talk."

"Did they find the dog?"

"Well, the police didn't, but one of the traffickers did. The dog was too weak to run a long way. The trafficker brought it by boat to Hastings."

"How many dogs did the gang have? And how many times did they use each dog?"

"It's difficult to say how many times they would use a dog. Eventually, each dog would become very weak and die. But several healthy Jack Russells were brought out of the flat."

"Why did they use dogs? Why didn't they just carry the heroin in a bag?"

"Because a bag can't run. These dogs were trained to run away if anyone said the word 'police'. Anyway, the police are now collecting evidence from the hidden cavern at the Smugglers Adventure."

The dogs wriggled in Joy's and Steve's arms each time they heard the word "police".

"So do we know who the mastermind is?" asked Joanna in the studio.

"Well, a Mrs Beth Skilling is in police custody in France. She was in the building here at the fishing beach yesterday, but the police allowed her to escape. They wanted to follow her and find out who she was working with in France. She drove straight to Folkestone and travelled through the Eurotunnel to Calais. The French police were waiting for her on the French side and they followed her in an unmarked car to a house near Calais. They didn't arrest her until she had parked the car and gone into the house."

"And you say she's in police custody in France now?"

"Yes, the police raided the house and found veterinary equipment along with a large quantity of heroin. They arrested Beth Skilling ..."

"Right, well, thank you, John. I'm sure we're going to hear a lot more on this story. But now over to tonight's other news ..."

As Steve picked up the remote control and pressed standby, the doorbell rang. Dave's dad went to answer it.

It was Trish, the vet. She followed Trevor into the living room and sat in an armchair. The two dogs came over and sat at her feet.

"Hello, Scruff. Hello, Coventry Patmore," she said. "Or maybe I should say: Hello, Tia. Hello, Charlie."

"What? Where did those names come from?" Steve asked.

"That's what they were called before, on their pet passports," said Trish. "The police found their passports at Natalie's flat. They also found their microchips."

"But only a vet can microchip dogs," said Steve.

"That's right," said Trish. "When I was on holiday in the spring, another vet stood in for me. Natalie told one of the drug traffickers to bring Tia and Charlie – I mean Scruff and Coventry Patmore – into the surgery. The trafficker brought them in and the vet vaccinated and microchipped the dogs. Anyway, Steve, the point is that all the dogs' papers are in order."

"Cool," said Steve.

"Yes, it really is cool. I was so worried, Steve. I thought we would have to put Scruff and Coventry Patmore to sleep. It's dangerous to keep dogs who may have rabies and other problems."

"Will Natalie go to prison?" asked Jack.

"Yes," said Trish. "The police said she's furious with herself. She's a very skilled animal nurse. But she was offered the chance to make a lot of money very fast. But even though she became greedy for money, she went on doing things the way she had been trained. She got the passports and microchips for the dogs in case they were seen at customs. Customs officers make random checks on cars. But then she changed her mind. She took out the microchips and kept them in her flat with the passports. She didn't want anyone to trace the dogs back to her."

"How strange," said Steve. "Natalie did everything perfectly, but then she put the dogs through such painful operations."

"Yes, she became too greedy," said Trish. "They all became greedier and greedier. They started by using one dog at a time. But then they decided that Natalie should operate on one dog in France while one of the men drove another dog to England. They thought that would double their money. But the driver couldn't manage without

Natalie in the car. He needed Natalie to keep the dog hidden ... Steve, what year are you in at school?"

"I'll be in Year 10 from September."

"Year 10 ... That's the year that does a week's work experience, isn't it?"

"Yes."

"Where do you want to do your work experience?"

"On a farm, maybe."

"Oh, right."

"Why?"

"Would you like to spend the week in my surgery? Have you thought about becoming a vet?"

"I think I'd like to be a farm vet, not a pets' vet. But I would like to come and help at your surgery and see what it's like. Thanks, Trish."

"You'll be a great vet," said Madeleine.

"I'll drink to that," said Dave's dad. "Help yourselves to drinks, everyone." He pointed to some bottles of beer, lemonade and cola on the mantelpiece.

He opened a bottle of beer and raised it in the air. "Here's to Steve's career as a vet. In fact, here's to all four of you – to Steve, Madeleine, Jack and Dave!"

"And to Scruff and Coventry Patmore," said Steve.

Vocabulary

Abbreviations
sb. = somebody; sth. = something;
jmdm. = jemandem; jmdn. = jemanden;
umg. = umgangssprachlich

A

(to) **abandon** [ə'bændən] verlassen
(to) **accuse** [ə'kjuːz] anklagen
addict ['ædɪkt] Abhängige(r)
alcove ['ælkəʊv] Alkoven; Nische
alleged [ə'ledʒd] mutmaßlich
anaesthetic [ˌænəs'θetɪk] Betäubungsmittel
ant [ænt] Ameise
anxious ['æŋkʃəs] beunruhigt
(to) **arrest** [ə'rest] verhaften, festnehmen
(to) **attempt** [ə'tempt] versuchen

B

backwards ['bækwədz] rückwärts
bead [biːd] Perle
beard [bɪəd]: **false beard** falscher Bart
bedside cabinet ['bedsaɪd 'kæbɪnət] Nachttisch, Nachtkästchen
belt [belt] Gürtel
bent [bent]: (to) **bend** beugen **(bend, bent, bent)**
beret ['bereɪ] Baskenmütze
biryani [ˌbɪri'ɑːni] *indisches Reisgericht*
boarding school ['bɔːdɪŋ skuːl] Internat
bolt [bəʊlt] (Schließ)riegel
(to) **bolt** verriegeln
bookcase ['bʊkkeɪs] Bücherregal
bound [baʊnd] gefesselt
bracelet ['breɪslət] Armband, Armreif
breath [breθ]: (to) **take a deep breath** tief einatmen
briefcase ['briːfkeɪs] Aktentasche
broom [bruːm] Besen
broomstick ['bruːmstɪk] Besenstiel
(to) **brush** [brʌʃ]: (to) **brush past sb.** jmdn. streifen
buckle ['bʌkl] Schnalle
bulge [bʌldʒ] Wulst

C

Caesarean [sɪ'zeəriən] Kaiserschnitt
cardboard ['kɑːdbɔːd] Karton, Pappe

cargo ['kɑːgəʊ] Fracht
carpet ['kɑːpɪt] Teppich
(to) **carve** [kɑːv] meißeln
cash desk ['kæʃ desk] Kasse, Kassenschalter
cavern ['kævən] *abgegrenzter Raum innerhalb einer Höhle*
cellar ['selə] Keller
chain [tʃeɪn] Kette; Fessel
chapel ['tʃæpl] Kapelle (*Andacht*)
charger ['tʃɑːdʒə] Ladegerät
cheek [tʃiːk] Wange
chemist's ['kemɪsts] Drogerie; Apotheke
chest [tʃest] Brust
chin [tʃɪn] Kinn
citizen ['sɪtɪzn] Staatsbürger(in)
(to) **clamber** ['klæmbə] klettern, kraxeln
coastguard ['kəʊstgɑːd] Küstenwache
coat [kəʊt] Mantel
concerned [kən'sɜːnd] besorgt
cordless ['kɔːdləs] schnurlos
(to) **cough** [kɒf] husten
council ['kaʊnsl]: **town council** Stadtrat
courtyard ['kɔːtjɑːd] (Innen)hof
crack [kræk] Riss, Sprung
(to) **crawl** [krɔːl] krabbeln; kriechen
(to) **creak** [kriːk] knarren
(to) **crouch** [kraʊtʃ] hocken; kauern
(to) **cuddle** ['kʌdl] knuddeln; schmusen
(to) **curl** [kɜːl]: (to) **curl round sb.** sich schützend um jmdn. legen
custody ['kʌstədi] Verwahrung
customer ['kʌstəmə] Kunde(-in)
customs ['kʌstəmz] Zoll

D

dagger ['dægə] Dolch
darkness ['dɑːknəs] Dunkelheit
daytime ['deɪtaɪm]: **in the daytime** tagsüber
(to) **defrost** [ˌdiː'frɒst] auftauen
delivery [dɪ'lɪvəri] Lieferung
direction [də'rekʃn] Richtung
(to) **drag** [dræg] ziehen; schleppen
drawer [drɔːə] Schublade
drunken ['drʌŋkən] betrunken
dug [dʌg]: (to) **dig into** eingraben **(dig, dug, dug)**
(to) **dump** [dʌmp] abladen; loswerden

E

edge [edʒ]: **water's edge** Ufer
(to) **edge** sich (vorbei)schleichen
elderly ['eldəli] ältere(r, -s)
(to) **empty** ['empti] leeren
engine ['endʒɪn] Motor
entrance ['entrəns] Eingang
envelope ['envələʊp] Briefumschlag
evidence ['evɪdəns] Beweis; Zeugenaussage

(to) **examine** [ɪg'zæmɪn] untersuchen
exit ['eksɪt] Ausgang

F

fake [feɪk] unecht
feather ['feðə] Feder
fingernail ['fɪŋgəneɪl] Fingernagel
fix [fɪks] *umg.* Schuss (*Drogen*)
(to) **flood** [flʌd] überschwemmen
folded ['fəʊldɪd] verschränkt; zusammengefaltet
fond [fɒnd]: (to) **be fond of sth.** etwas mögen
footstep ['fʊtstep] Schritt
foster carer ['fɒstə 'keərə] *Person, die sich um elternlose Kinder kümmert*
frame [freɪm]: **door frame** Türrahmen
(to) **frown** [fraʊn] die Stirn runzeln
fur [fɜː] Fell

G

gag [gæg] Knebel
gagged geknebelt
garlic ['gɑːlɪk] Knoblauch
gently ['dʒentli] behutsam
gibbet ['dʒɪbɪt] Galgen
grain [greɪn]: **grain of sand** Sandkörnchen
(to) **groan** [grəʊn] stöhnen (*Schmerzen*)
grown-up ['grəʊn ʌp] Erwachsene(r)
(to) **grunt** [grʌnt] ächzen; grunzen
guide dog ['gaɪd dɒg] Blindenhund

H

habit ['hæbɪt]: (to) **make a habit of sth.** etwas zur Gewohnheit werden lassen
(to) **handcuff sb.** ['hændkʌf] jmdm. Handschellen anlegen
handle ['hændl] (Tür)klinke; Griff
haunted ['hɔːntɪd]: **it's haunted** es spukt (dort)
headland ['hedlənd] Landspitze
headquarters [ˌhed'kwɔːtəz] Zentrale; Hauptquartier
heavy ['hevi] schwer
hedge [hedʒ] Hecke
high-heeled [ˌhaɪ'hiːld] hochhackig
hooded ['hʊdɪd] mit Kapuze
hoodie ['hʊdi] Kapuzenpullover; -jacke
hook [hʊk] Haken

I

(to) **identify** [aɪ'dentɪfaɪ] identifizieren
(to) **involve** [ɪn'vɒlv] betreffen

J

jangling ['dʒæŋglɪŋ]: **jangling sound** rasselndes Geräusch
jewellery ['dʒuːəlri] Schmuck
jumper ['dʒʌmpə] Pullover

K

(to) **key in** [ˌkiːˈɪn] eingeben, eintippen
knot [nɒt] Knoten

L

lamb korma [læm ˈkɔːmə] *indisches Currygericht mit Lammfleisch*
lap [læp] Schoß
(to) **lap** auflecken, aufschlecken
(to) **lean** [liːn]: (to) **lean forward** sich vorbeugen
(to) **lean over sth.** sich über etwas beugen
limply [lɪmpli] kraftlos
lipstick [ˈlɪpstɪk] Lippenstift
log [lɒg] Holzscheit
low-cut [ˌləʊˈkʌt] tief ausgeschnitten

M

maniac [ˈmeɪniæk] Verrückte(r), Irre(r)
mantelpiece [ˈmæntlpiːs] Kaminsims
mastermind [ˈmɑːstəmaɪnd] führender Kopf
(to) **match** [mætʃ] zusammenpassen
memory [ˈmeməri] Erinnerung
(to) **moan** [məʊn] *umg.* jammern
moustache [məˈstɑːʃ]: **droopy moustache** nach unten hängender Schnurrbart
mouthful [ˈmaʊθfʊl] Bissen, Mundvoll
muffled [ˈmʌfld] gedämpft; leise
mulberry [ˈmʌlbəri]: **mulberry tree** Maulbeerbaum

N

nail [neɪl] (Finger)nagel
narrow [ˈnærəʊ] schmal, eng
newborn [ˈnjuːbɔːn] neugeboren
notebook [ˈnəʊtbʊk] Notizbuch
(to) **nudge** [nʌdʒ] (an)stoßen; (an)stupsen
(to) **nuzzle** [ˈnʌzl] ankuscheln

O

oar [ɔː] Ruder
(to) **operate** [ˈɒpəreɪt] operieren

P

packaging [ˈpækɪdʒɪŋ] Verpacken, Einpacken
padlock [ˈpædlɒk] Vorhängeschloss
pagan [ˈpeɪgən] heidnisch
painful [ˈpeɪnfl] schmerzhaft
palm [pɑːm] Handfläche
passageway [ˈpæsɪdʒweɪ] (Durch)gang
passport [ˈpɑːspɔːt] (Reise)pass
patch [pætʃ] Fleck
patio [ˈpætiəʊ] Terrasse
paw [pɔː] Pfote
payment [ˈpeɪmənt] Zahlung, Bezahlung
(to) **peep out** [ˌpiːpˈaʊt] herausgucken

pebble ['pebl] Kieselstein
pile [paɪl] Stapel
pint [paɪnt] *Maßeinheit*
1 Pint = 0,57 l
(to) **place** [pleɪs] legen
(to) **plead** [pliːd] (an)flehen
(to) **plug into** [ˌplʌg'ɪntu] angeschlossen sein
pot [pɒt] Kanne
(to) **pour** [pɔː] (ein)gießen
powder ['paʊdə] Pulver
prawn [prɔːn] Garnele, Krabbe
pregnant ['pregnənt] schwanger (*Person*); trächtig (*Tier*)
prescription [prɪ'skrɪpʃn] Rezept (*Medizin*)
(to) **press** [pres] drücken
protection [prə'tekʃn] Schutz
puppy ['pʌpi] Welpe
pure [pjʊə] rein

Q

quantity ['kwɒntəti] Menge
(to) **question** ['kwestʃən] befragen; vernehmen

R

rabies ['reɪbiːz] Tollwut
rags [rægz] Lumpen
raid [reɪd] Razzia
(to) **raid** durchsuchen
random ['rændəm]: **random check** Stichprobe (*Grenzkontrolle*)
rather ['rɑːðə] lieber
reassured [ˌriːə'ʃʊəd]: (to) **feel reassured** sich gestärkt fühlen
receipt [rɪ'siːt] Kassenbon, Quittung
recipe ['resəpi] Rezept (*Essen*)
refugee [ˌrefjʊ'dʒiː] Flüchtling
(to) **refuse** [rɪ'fjuːz] verweigern
rejected [rɪ'dʒektɪd] zurückgewiesen
remains [rɪ'meɪnz] (Über)reste
remote control [rɪˌməʊtkən'trəʊl] Fernbedienung
(to) **remove** [rɪ'muːv] entfernen
replacement [rɪ'pleɪsmənt] Nachfolger(in); Ersatz
(to) **rescue** ['reskjuː] retten
(to) **rest** [rest] (an)lehnen; ruhen
(to) **return** [rɪ'tɜːn] zurückkommen, wiederkommen
(to) **reveal** [rɪ'viːl] enthüllen; zeigen
rib [rɪb] Rippe
rid [rɪd]: (to) **get rid of sth.** etwas loswerden
rifle range ['raɪfl reɪndʒ] Schießstand
rough [rʌf] rauh
(to) **row** [raʊ] rudern

S

scale [skeɪl]: **weighing scale** Waage
(to) **scare** [skeə] erschrecken
scarf [skɑːf] Schal (*Plural* **scarves**)
(to) **secure** [sɪ'kjʊə] festbinden; sichern
shore [ʃɔː] Ufer

sighted ['saɪtɪd]: **sighted people** *Menschen, die sehen können*
silk [sɪlk] Seide
(to) **sip** [sɪp] (in kleinen Schlucken) trinken
skeleton ['skelɪtn] Skelett
skilled [skɪld] ausgebildet
slinky ['slɪŋki] aufreizend
(to) **slip** [slɪp] (aus)rutschen
(to) **slither** ['slɪðə] schlittern
smelt [smelt]: (to) **smell** riechen **(smell, smelt, smelt)**
smuggler ['smʌglə] Schmuggler(in)
(to) **sneeze** [sniːz] niesen
(to) **sniff** [snɪf] schnüffeln; riechen
soaking wet [ˌsəʊkɪŋ'wet] klatschnass
socket ['sɒkɪt] Steckdose
soluble ['sɒljəbl] löslich
spare [speə] Ersatz
sparrow ['spærəʊ] Spatz, Sperling
spell [spel]: (to) **cast a spell on sb.** jmdn. verhexen
spiked-up [ˌspaɪkt'ʌp]: **spiked-up hair** hochgegelte Haare
spooky ['spuːki] *umg.* gespenstisch, unheimlich
(to) **squint** [skwɪnt] blinzeln
(to) **stab** [stæb] erstechen
(to) **stagger** ['stægə] taummeln, schwanken
stair [steə] (Treppen)stufe
stall [stɔːl] Stand
stitch [stɪtʃ]: **row of stitches** genähte Wunde
sticker ['stɪkə] Aufkleber
strode [strəʊd]: (to) **stride** schreiten **(stride, strode, stridden)**
(to) **stroke** [strəʊk] streicheln
(to) **struggle** ['strʌgl] sich abmühen
supply [sə'plaɪ] Vorrat
surgery ['sɜːdʒəri] (Arzt)praxis
surgical ['sɜːdʒɪkl] chirurgisch
(to) **suspect** [sə'spekt] verdächtigen; vermuten
(to) **swallow** ['swɒləʊ] (hinunter)schlucken
(to) **switch off** [ˌswɪtʃ'ɒf] ausschalten (*Gerät*)
(to) **switch on** [ˌswɪtʃ'ɒn] einschalten (*Gerät*)
sword [sɔːd] Schwert

T

tail [teɪl] Schwanz
(to) **tap** [tæp]: (to) **tap sb. on the shoulder** jmdm. auf die Schulter tippen
thick [θɪk] dick
thin [θɪn] dünn
(to) **throb** [θrɒb] pochen
tide [taɪd]: **low tide** Ebbe
tissue ['tɪʃuː,'tɪsjuː] Papiertaschentuch
toenail ['təʊneɪl] Zehennagel
(to) **top up** [ˌtɒp'ʌp] aufladen (*Handyguthaben*)
torch [tɔːtʃ] Taschenlampe
trafficker ['træfɪkə]: **drug trafficker** Drogenhändler(in)
traitor ['treɪtə] Verräter(in)

(to) **trip** [trɪp]: (to) **trip over** stolpern
tray [treɪ] Tablett

U

(to) **unlock** [ˌʌn'lɒk] aufschließen
unmarked [ʌn'mɑːkt]: **unmarked car** Zivilfahrzeug der Polizei
unsteadily [ʌn'stedili] wackelig
(to) **untie** [ʌn'taɪ] aufmachen; losbinden
(to) **unzip** [ˌʌn'zɪp]: (to) **unzip sth.** den Reißverschluss von etwas aufmachen
updated [ˌʌp'deɪtɪd]: (to) **keep sb. updated** jmdn. auf dem Laufenden halten
upwards ['ʊpwədz] nach oben
urgently ['ɜːdʒəntli] eindringlich

V

(to) **vaccinate** ['væksɪneɪt] impfen
(to) **vanish** ['vænɪʃ] verschwinden
vet [vet] Tierarzt(-ärztin)
(to) **vomit** ['vɒmɪt] sich übergeben

W

(to) **wag** [wæg]: (to) **wag frantically** wild wedeln
waxwork ['wækswɜːk] Wachsfigur
wedding ['wedɪŋ]: **wedding day** Hochzeitstag
wheelie bin ['wiːli bɪn] *Mülltonne mit Rädern*
(to) **whimper** ['wɪmpə] wimmern
(to) **whine** [waɪn] winseln (*Hund*)
wicked ['wɪkɪd] gemein; boshaft
witch [wɪtʃ] Hexe
womb [wuːm] Gebärmutter, Mutterleib
wooden ['wʊdn] hölzern, Holz-
wrecked [rekt] zerstört; schiffbrüchig

Y

yelp [jelp] Gebell; Gejaule

Z

zip [zɪp] Reißverschluss

Check your understanding

Chapter 1

1 Who lives next door to Jack?
2 What advice does Joy give Jack?

Chapter 2

1 Where does Dave's dad work?
2 What is Dave doing in the souvenir shop?

Chapter 3

1 What did Dave hear in the caves in the morning?
2 Why is Steve in a hurry to get out of the caves?

Chapter 4

1 How can Dave's mum see everyone going in and out of the caves?
2 Why does Madeleine want to go to Jack's house?

Chapter 5

1 Why can't Jack and Madeleine get into the living room?
2 What dropped out of Beth's pocket?

Chapter 6

1 What did Dave feel with his foot?
2 What does Jack keep in the passageway?

Chapter 7

1 What did the American tourists want?
2 Why did Lady Macbeth put some of the dead king's blood on the guards' swords?

Chapter 8

1 Which two places are people flashing lights from?

Chapter 9

1 Describe the man with the dog.
2 Describe the dog.

Chapter 10

1 What is different about the dog today?
2 Why does Steve ask if the dog has had a Caesarean?

Chapter 11

1 What did someone pull through the opening into the Smugglers Adventure?
2 What does Steve want to find?

Chapter 12

1 Where did they find the dog?
2 How did the man fall down?

Chapter 13

1 Who held the dog close to him on the cliff lift?

Chapter 14

1 Why did Dave decide to explore the cavern on his hands and knees?
2 What did Dave find in the cavern?

Chapter 15

1 Why does Joy think Scruff hasn't had a Caesarean?
2 When Jack looked up at his dad's bedroom window, who was looking down at him?

Chapter 16

1 The dog with the patch of black fur on its back was frightened. How do we know this?

2 Why are there no other boats on the sea?

Chapter 17

1 How did Jack know the light wasn't from a fishing boat?

Chapter 18

1 What did the fishermen find on the beach?

2 Why can't the new dog be pregnant?

Chapter 19

1 What did Madeleine put under the blanket?

Chapter 20

1 What did Jack find in his jeans pocket?

2 Why are they going to call the new dog Coventry Patmore?

Chapter 21

1 What's on the bookcase in the hidden cavern?

2 Why does Dave tell Jack to put his torch off?

Chapter 22

1 Describe the sticker on the Frenchman's sports bag.

2 What did the men do with Jack, Dave and Madeleine?

Chapter 23

1 Who is Scruff frightened of?

2 Scruff runs whenever anyone says this word. What is it?

Chapter 24

1 What were the men carrying when they left the caves?

2 What did Dave have under his jumper?

Chapter 25

1 What did Jack see on Beth's handbag?

2 What was the piece of paper that Jack had found?

Chapter 26

1 What did they find in the briefcase?

2 What is Beth's surname?

Chapter 27

1 Molly saw four people go into a building near the fishing beach. Who were they?

2 Where was Molly sitting?

Chapter 28

1 What did the vet find when she operated on Coventry Patmore's stomach?

2 Why did she need police officers with her when she operated?

Chapter 29

1 What does Jack want to do?

Chapter 30

1 How far from Hastings is the Eurotunnel port at Folkestone?

2 Where would the drug smugglers collect their payments?

Chapter 31

1 Why did the police allow Beth to escape?

2 What kind of vet would Steve like to be?